To Brother Tom Brackeen
with best wishes and hope
that the most resourceful blacks
will come together in a well-
organized effort and help
accelerate the personal development and social progress of
substantially more young
African Americans.

Brother Elliott Dorian Gadsden
Feb. 18, 1991.

Progress against the Tide

E. Dorian Gadsden

VANTAGE PRESS
New York / Los Angeles / Chicago

In memory of my father
and dedicated to my beloved wife
and our two sons

Contents

Chapter IV. Segregation in Practice   **54**

Chapter V. Discrimination in Practice   **77**

Chapter VI. Desegregation—Litigation   **106**

Acknowledgments

I would like to express my appreciation to the librarians in the Moreland Collection at Howard University, the librarians at Martin Luther King, Jr. Library, and the Library of Congress Section on periodicals on microfilm for their cordial assistance when called upon.

I am deeply indebted to Ms. Mattie L. Townsend for her dependable assistance to me in the research of much of this work, and to Mrs. Bettye J. Harris for her responsible typing of the entire manuscript and the many revisions occasioned for its completion.

Finally, I am indeed very grateful to Mrs. Persephone L. Brown and Mr. Ricardo H. Harris for critically reading and sugggesting editorial changes in several portions of this work.

Introduction

The struggle of black Americans for freedom from bondage and various forms of racial segregation and discrimination imposed by law had been in progress for over 349 years (1619–1968). During all of those years in America, however, their struggle has been upstream, against a strong tide of racial oppression by law and tradition. It was not until the years 1955–1968 that Americans witnessed the first massive coordinated and sustained solidarity effort of blacks to obtain substantial freedom and citizenship. The long collaborative struggle of black leaders, civil rights organizations, and their white and black allies during that period may properly be described as the thrust of the civil rights movement in the United States. The struggle continued with increasing intensity until the enactment of the civil rights acts of 1964 and 1965 by the Congress and the untimely assassination of the principal leader of the movement, Dr. Martin Luther King, Jr., on April 4, 1968. The Fair Housing Act became law a few months after his death.

The National Association for the Advancement of Colored People (NAACP), the Urban League, and other organizations continue their vigilant efforts to this day to secure and protect the constitutional rights and privileges of blacks. However, the passage of the civil rights acts and the assassination of Dr. King were essentially the anticlimax of the massive movement. Corresponding with the decline of the movement was the absence of a clear sense of direction as well as an appropriate private and coordinated efficacy to accelerate the personal development and progress of blacks in general. Such an efficacy by blacks probably never evolved because many blacks, like many other Americans, thought everything would fall in place with the passage of the civil rights acts. However, most blacks have since learned that was not true.

Certainly, a substantial number of blacks pursued and profited from the newly won civil rights laws and programs, such as equal employment opportunity and affirmative action, small business loans from the Small Business Administration, guaranteed student loans for education, manpower development and training for various job occupations, and the GI Bill of Rights for veterans of the military services. Many of these blacks have since achieved affluence and respectability for themselves. Responding to the norms of human nature to aspire for greater progress and success, many of them moved to more affluent neighborhoods, often among members of the larger society. Their departure from the less affluent black environment often resulted in a breach in their intimate contact or relationship with the black community.

By 1975, the steady stream of leadership and resourcefulness of many achieved blacks away from the black community left a void of appropriate direction and leadership for constructive progress for a larger number of blacks. Many among the masses of blacks left behind were seen floundering in bewilderment, seeking an undefined identity, manifesting a negative and often belligerent attitude towards achieved blacks and whites, while lacking an adequate knowledge of their own historical heritage to help explain the plight and existing level of progress of American blacks. Consequently, the period from 1975 to the present has been characterized by some blacks as a period of economic and cultural impasse, if not retrogression, for many blacks. It was common to read newspaper columns or to hear radio and television commentators, live public figures and rank-and-file citizens asking—where is the black leadership—what happened to the black movement—is the plight of blacks getting worse, and if so, what are blacks doing about it?

Middle-class blacks are frequently accused of deserting black communities and the plight of the people there. They are often accused of failing to engage in constructive and supportive action to improve the well-being of those culturally imprisoned in ignorance, poverty, and criminally infested ghettos of many cities. The black middle class is defined in many ways and for many purposes. However, in keeping with the notion of reasonable social progress associated with self-sufficiency, education, income, and middle Americans' life style, "middle-class blacks," for purposes of this writing, is defined as follows:

The approximately 25–30 percent of black family heads of household, having 12 or more years of formal education, or full occupational training, with an annual income of $20,000 to $35,000, as well as the minority of blacks with earnings in excess of $35,000.

For further discussion on what constitutes "middle-class blacks," see: *The Myth of Black Progress,* by Alphonso Pinkney (Cambridge: Cambridge University Press, 1985), pp. 99–103.

While the earlier assertion about middle-class blacks correctly notes a conspicuous absence of many of them living in the black community, it probably overstates the lack of actual involvement and concern of many of them. It manifestly overlooks the substantial number of them still working in public and private institutions and agencies in the black community. These blacks (teachers, social workers, church and civic community workers, recreation and drug abuse workers, business operators and police and fire personnel) often do not live in the black community. They are not always visible in the black community, although their work, concerns, efforts, and sometimes their money are of direct or indirect benefit to the black community. It would be a gross oversight not to recognize the presence and contributions of these blacks, although their contributions fall far short of the necessary demands of the black community.

Nevertheless, the frequent accusations about the lack of concern of middle-class blacks call attention to several questions about their validity, or reasons for their invalidity. Perhaps middle-class blacks should be asked whether they are noncaring and indifferent to the plight of less fortunate blacks in general. An appropriate way to elicit an answer to this question might be to ask them if they have any blood relatives, friends, or loved ones still struggling in poverty and ignorance. If the answer is in the affirmative, as one might suspect a substantial number would be, an appropriate follow-up question could be whether they care about the plight of such relatives, friends, or loved ones. Perhaps the final question could be whether the experiences of middle-class blacks in American life have been so comforting that they see no need to identify with, or to be genuinely concerned about, the masses of less fortunate blacks.

While the answers to the latter questions will be left to speculation of the reader, the writer has personally observed that at
nearly any gathering of middle-class blacks, where reasonable
circumstances and time permit, invariably their conversations result in some discussion about the status or rate of progress of
blacks in general. They seem to concur that continued, meaningful, and significant progress for black Americans means blacks
must not only acquire a good education (high school, college, and
above), but also a socially acceptable degree of personal development—cultural refinement—as well. They seem to perceive "personal development" in the aggregate to include:

1. A positive attitude toward learning and supervision.
2. Respectable behavior—courteousness—good manners.
3. Reasonable articulation and writing of standard English.
4. Responsible and dependable work habits—punctuality.
5. Seriousness of purpose appropriate to the endeavor.
6. Self-esteem and motivation.
7. Efforts to cultivate appealing, as distinguished from offensive
   and hostile, personalities.

All of such qualities tend to enhance the social progress of any
American.

While both formal education and refined acculturation have
been somewhat overlapping processes, except for some private
finishing schools, education in this country has been essentially
a function of the school, and cultural refinement a function of the
family in its environmental setting. However, when we examine
the history of educational opportunity for blacks in America and
the disruptive historical impact of slavery and racial discrimination
on their organized family life, we gain some insight into the problems and some understanding of the current status and behavior
of American blacks.

It appears to be willingly conceded by many Americans that
the progress of blacks following the Civil Rights Acts of the 1960s
was meaningful and substantial. It was refreshing for those who
observed or enjoyed such progress after so many years of lawful
and traditional racial discrimination which restrained the general
progress of blacks. However, in approximately 1970, it became

evident that such progress, and the prospect for continued significant progress, were being diminished to some degree by a variety of contemporary factors in the American society:

(1) Coinciding with the continued increase in the black population were dynamic changes in the economy, brought about by automation, cybernation, the debt of the Vietnam War, American entrepreneurs moving their business operations abroad for cheaper labor and larger profits, the progressive increase of women leaving the home and entering the work force, the substantial increase in immigrants especially from Latin America and Asia, causing a significant increase in job competition; a significant decline in American foreign trade, inflation, the oil embargo of November 1973, and the consequential effects of all of these changes; residual racial discrimination in employment and promotion opportunities; the ever increasing national debt, and finally, the policies of President Reagan's administration to deal with inflation, the budget deficit, and efforts to substantially reduce affirmative action in employment. Thus, the quality and availability of many kinds of jobs became scarce and requirements for other jobs, more difficult for many Americans, especially for a substantial number of blacks.
(2) There has also been a substantial increase in disorganization of American families by divorce and separation, and for a while, a significant decrease in marriages. Blacks being a part of the total American culture were no less adversely affected by these national trends. Thus, the pre-existing disorganization in black families was therefore compounded, since a large percentage of them had not yet recovered from the family disorganization occasioned by slavery and many years of economic repression—discrimination in employment.

One can observe along with the accelerated disorganiztion in black families the cultural waste of many black youths, especially the black male. There are far too many black males overflowing our prisons, drug abuse centers, permanently unemployed, and recipients of the welfare program. There are also far too many other black males trailing the class in junior and senior high school, if not dropping out, and irresponsibly roaming the streets, developing the wrong set of values. Indeed, it is impossible to disassociate this chaotic quality of human development from the numerous social ills of blacks, including a substantial rise in teenage pregnancies and female heads of household struggling to support children, in numerous cases, independent of any paternal assistance.

The educational and cultural gap between black men and women continues to grow. Many black girls are excelling black boys in personal development and achievement by a significant degree, and frequently finding themselves at the young adult stage in life, searching desperately for a comparable black mate. The failure to reverse this growing educational and cultural disparity between black men and women is a foregone conclusion of what the current trend will do to future marriages, fatherhood, the black family, black male-female relations, as well as to the social orientation of children and their personal development.

With this general state of affairs, many middle-class blacks are understandably confounded as to what they can do individually about the astronomical social problems confronting the black population in this country. A large number of them have expressed the belief that the problems of the black community—progress for blacks in general—are overwhelming and beyond their individual capacity to make any meaningful contribution to their resolution or relief. Some middle-class blacks manifest an indifference to problems peculiar to blacks and a few pretend such problems do not exist. Understandably, other middle-class blacks would like very much to be of assistance, but only in an endeavor that is likely to produce substantial and meaningful progress.

Still other middle-class blacks, who are not snobs by any means, are reluctant to step forward and become involved in an unstructured, uncoordinated endeavor, and offer their leadership, expertise and wisdom, only to be disrespected, humiliated, hated, and possibly assaulted by some blacks who manifest an anti-achieved attitude towards well-educated and sophisticated blacks. Although some middle-class blacks have done much to induce this attitude by other blacks, it is surmised that the substantial majority of them have not done anything to encourage such negativism towards themselves. All of these attitudes raise the question: Can blacks substantially accelerate the progress of blacks in general? Irrespective of the diversity of attitudes towards substantial black progress, a cooperative effort for progress will require both genuine and able leadership by middle-class blacks, as well as cooperative followership by blacks for whom such an effort is designed to help.

There may be some justification for all of the attitudes of middle-class blacks towards black progress in the absence of a comprehensive and well-coordinated efficacy designed to result in substantial and meaningful progress for blacks in general. If such a program presently exists, evidently it is not a matter of common knowledge. Perhaps the litmus test for challenging the willingness, interest, and genuine concern of middle-class blacks to substantially improve the general well being of blacks is to provide a well-designed plan for personal development. Tap middle-class blacks on the shoulder and challenge them to accept the responsibility of assisting in carrying out the task to be performed. The writer is fairly confident that a substantial majority of blacks, along with some whites and other Americans, will assist in such an undertaking.

The object of this writing was conceived within the context of this sociological state of affairs of blacks. Although the author does not have a designed efficacy for black progress in his pocket, as perhaps no single individual has, he does have and will submit in this writing an approach for the development of a program to salvage many black youths and hopefully accelerate the personal development and progress of many others.

However, entertaining any thought of prognosis or remedy to address the social growth and progress of many blacks without a brief review and analysis of the socio-historical background of them would be comparable to a physician prescribing medication for a patient without physical examination. Nor will the reader appreciate a discussion of such an approach without reading the historical background in each of the chapters in this volume. Such an analysis might prove helpful to many blacks and other Americans in understanding, at least in part, why the general status of blacks is where it is in current America. Such an analysis appears compelling in view of the numerous and recent commentaries by black and white public figures, and even some purported social scientists to the effect that blacks can no longer blame their current status on slavery and past outlawed racial segregation and discrimination. Some exponents of that point of view have even compared the arrival and progress of black Americans with the arrival and progress of other ethnic groups in America.

It should be willingly conceded that blacks in general cannot objectively attribute all of the ills of their current status to slavery and past racial discrimination. However, neither can it be honestly maintained that the long and desolate nightmare of slavery and legalized segregation and discrimination did not have a substantial adverse effect upon black families, their progress, and their current general status in America. What percentage such an impact has had is left for the reader to assess. The primary purpose of a brief historical analysis is to set forth a part of the record which significantly contributed to the current status of blacks, and more importantly, to afford some insight into an approach for the development of an essential approach to salvage some blacks from cultural waste and enhance the social progress of many others.

The socio-historical presentation related in the following chapters is not designed to develop chronic and negative feelings about the past by blacks, but hopefully to aid them and other Americans in understanding in part the current social status of American blacks. It is designed to cause blacks to have an appreciation for the endurance and survival of their ancestors, as well as to encourage a willingness among present generations of them to join hands with other genuine Americans in working to accelerate the social progress of many more blacks. Nothing in this volume was designed to be offensive or embarrassing to any group or organization. It is intended, however, to be thought-provoking—to generate intelligent and informed dialogue and encourage the advancement of constructive ideas and progressive action—to accelerate the overall progress of blacks and enhance race relations in America.

It should be recognized that this brief background of blacks on the few pages in this volume could not possibly serve as a comprehensive all-inclusive history of American blacks. Indeed, it was not so intended. Nor can it do justice to the long and severe suffering of the ancestors of blacks, or to the comprehensive and scholarly works of the several authors, cited and not cited, in history and sociology, who researched and assembled the events of slavery long after it was abolished.

Much has been written about slavery, racial discrimination, and other aspects of black history. However, the writer is indeed very grateful that an abundance of various aspects of black history and sociology, for purposes of this writing, was readily available in the excellent works of such scholarly authors as Carter G. Woodson, Gunnar Myrdal, Kenneth M. Stampp, John Hope Franklin, E. Franklin Frazier, Brewton Berry, Lerone Bennett, Jr., Andrew Billingsley, A. Leon Higginbotham, Jr., Doris Y. Wilkinson and Ronald Taylor, and many others cited in the footnotes, as well as other scholars who preceded or followed them. For a more comprehensive knowledge of the historical and sociological subjects on American blacks, the reader is referred to the authoritative sources in the notes after each chapter. Americans owe a debt of gratitude to all of them.

One   Prelude to Chattel Slavery

The Origin of Slave Trading in the New World

The origin of Negro slavery in America can be traced to the earliest history of Africa and other continents where slavery was widespread. Although African slavery was cruel and oppressive, as it was elsewhere, its premise was not always mono-racial but included persons of different racial or ethnic heritage. Generally, slaves were treated much like servants until the downfall of feudalism and the concurrent onset of the commercial revolution which brought about the rise of influential states like Spain, Portugal, France, Britain, and Holland.[1]

In the early seventeenth century, the islands in the West Indies were controlled by Spain, and the Dutch West India Company, with the support of its government, promoted a lucrative business in the Caribbean slave trade. However, when Denmark, Holland, France and England acquired territory in the area, need arose for labor in developing the New World in the West Indies. Since slavery was a revenue-producing system, the islands became the object of European diplomacy and a valuable new source of revenue for Europe. Consequently, the competition for wealth derived from human trading first pursued by the Dutch and Portuguese was then pursued by the French and English traders. As the new plantations in the islands expanded, so did the slave-trading business.

The importation of African slaves into the West Indies in 1540 was estimated at ten thousand. As the human-trading business grew, the Dutch, French, and English companies acquired dominance in the competition. The King of England chartered the Royal

African Company in 1672, which enabled it to assume dominance of the slave-trading industry for the next half century. Trading posts or factories were established on the coast of Africa to facilitate the trading of African slaves for guns, gunpowder, ivory, whiskey, brandy, rum, and a variety of foods.[2]

When captured, African males and females were taken away from their families either by deceptive schemes or physical force of slave traders. They were chained together, and with clubs or weapons, forcibly marched for days or weeks over miles of land to the trading posts or stations on the coast of Africa. There, they were imprisoned for weeks as they waited to become cargo on the first available slave vessel enroute to the New World. As Franklin observes, the slave traders traded for the healthiest, youngest, largest, ablest, and most culturally advanced males, primarily from West Africa, depriving the continent of an invaluable resource. As the slaves were taken aboard the trading ships, they grieved deeply over leaving their families and country. Franklin reports how one slave trader stated Negroes were "so willful and loathed to leave their own country that they have often leaped out of the canoes, boats and ships, into the sea, and kept under water until they were drowned." To avoid the horrors of the voyage and enslavement in a distant land, many slaves would leap off the ship into the mouth of a shark.[3]

The Voyage to the New World

The voyage by vessels to the New World, called the "Middle Passage," represents perhaps the most inhuman and barbaric conditions in human history under which man has ever transported man by force. It was undertaken with the slaves chained together, lying side by side as timber stacked on shelves, one above the other, on both sides of an aisle down the middle of the ship, without any individual provisions for human elimination. The guards could walk the aisles and flog the chained slaves to keep order. The number of slaves aboard the vessel exceeded the capacity for comfort to allow for the loss of slaves occasioned by the conditions of the long voyage. As the weeks and months duration of the voyage progressed, the stench and unsanitary conditions greatly increased incidents of disease and epidemics such as smallpox and the deadly flu, which accounted for an increase in the mortality rate of the slaves. By the time the ships reached their destination in the West Indies or the American colonies, that rate would have further increased as a result of hunger strikes, which made the slaves more susceptible to disease. Many slaves who survived death by disease and suicide were often permanently impaired from disease or maimed from their resistance and movement against the shackles and chains.[4]

Slaves in the New World

Phillip D. Curtin estimated there were 9,566,100 slaves imported from Africa to the New World between 1451 and 1870, representing great wealth to the Europeans and those entrepreneurs engaged in the slave trade. The slaves were used to clear the land and till the fields in developing a lucrative agricultural economy, first growing tobacco and later, after England gained dominance in the West Indies, sugar cane.

The mortality rate among newly arrived slaves was as high as 30 percent during the three or four seasoning years. Such deaths resulted mostly from the new change of climate, new diseases, suicide, exposure incurred in running away, and excessive flogging by landlords in breaking slaves in to their new environment. Slave overseers made no distinction between males and females with respect to work requirements or flogging for dereliction of duty. Slaves worked long days, and during the harvest season, as much as eighteen hours. Pregnant women were forced to work until the time of birth and the maximum time allowed for recovery was one month.

After the Caribbean Islands became almost overpopulated, there appeared to be no substantial increase in the slave population as a result of human reproduction until their emancipation in 1830. The death rate among the slaves there was extraordinarily high, suggesting they were grossly mistreated. The excessive degree of inhumanity to the slaves in the West Indies is attributed in part to the prosperous absentee landlordism (English and Spanish entrepreneurs) of the system. To those landlords, the islands were a source of wealth but not a place of residence. Their only concern with affairs and well-being of people in the islands was production of wealth. Franklin concluded that the mistreatment of slaves by overseers in the islands is unparalleled in the history of slavery. However, as prosperity in the West Indies declined in the early eighteenth century, Europeans turned their attention and interest to North American colonies and many slaves were exported from the West Indies into American colonies.[5]

Most grade school pupils in American history learn early that in 1620 the Pilgrims, in search of religious freedom, brighter hopes, and a better life, voluntarily landed at Plymouth Rock in what is now Plymouth, Massachusetts. However, few grade-school pupils learn that one year earlier, twenty blacks were brought to Jamestown, Virginia, in late August 1619, by a Dutchman who sold them to colonists in search of a larger labor force. These blacks, unlike the Pilgrims, were brought unwillingly in chains with force of violence as captives seized from a Spanish slave ship. They represented the first end of the thread of black servitude and slavery established in colonial America.[6]

The first blacks brought to colonial America in the seventeenth century served largely as servants without a definite term of service. They worked and mingled socially with white indentured servants. Although the character of the servitude of blacks at that time was not clear, it eventually evolved into a servitude similar to that of a lower-level white indentured servant. Indentured servants were persons—mostly white, poor, and/or convicts—who voluntarily came or were brought to the colonies bound by contract to serve a master for a specified number of years—usually seven. After the term of years expired, the indentured servant would have earned, or was allowed to purchase his or her freedom. Most of the first twenty blacks in Jamestown were eventually allowed to become free persons.[7] Prior to chattel slavery (slaves deemed and treated as "personal property," as distinguished from term or perpetual indentured servants), servitude, as defined by practice, varied to some extent from colony to colony. Nonetheless, with few exceptions, blacks generally could not earn or purchase

4

their freedom after a term of years in service.[8] Nor were they generally free to marry, testify in court, or own property like white indentured servants.[9]

Initially, colonies most deeply involved in the importation of slaves were Virginia (the embryo of institutionalized slavery), Delaware, Maryland, North Carolina, South Carolina, and Pennsylvania, with Virginia setting the pace and shaping the character and form of the system.[10] Slave traders also operated and slavery existed on a minuscule scale in Newport and Providence, Rhode Island, as well as Salem and Boston, Massachusetts. Massachusetts was the first colony to legally abolish slavery in 1641. By legislative enactment, Georgia, which had been relatively humane towards slavery compared to other colonies, legally sanctioned slavery in 1750.[11]

"One by one, Kentucky, Tennessee, Mississippi and Alabama entered the Union as slave states," while the institution had already existed in Louisiana and Florida by virtue of the purchase of those regions from France. Missouri and Arkansas inherited the institution, having been carved out of the Florida-Louisiana regions. When Texas was annexed in 1845, slave labor became a part of its culture. These colonies constituted the fifteen states in which slavery existed as a substantial system of labor.[12]

In 1649 the number of blacks in Virginia had slowly risen to only three hundred, and southern landholders were utilizing white labor until the end of the seventeenth century, when English and colonial merchants entered the slave trade. Subsequently, thousands of blacks were imported annually from Africa and the West Indies during the eighteenth century. Just prior to the onset of the American Revolution, the population of Virginia was nearly evenly divided between whites and blacks, while blacks in South Carolina outnumbered whites by two to one.[13]

As importation of slaves increased throughout the colonies, there was no clear distinction between servitude and slavery. This state of ambiguity existed for forty-one years, until the Virginia legislature further clarified the status of blacks by statutory acknowledgment of their perpetual bondage in 1660, and the blacks were ultimately debased from quasi-indentured servants to slaves. Prior to this time (1619–1660), the labor force was composed of whites and blacks of various degrees of servitude. However, as the number of blacks in lifetime bondage increased, the labor force constituted totally enslaved blacks, while indentured servants and black servants worked side by side. As a result of such intimate relations, white-black alliances for escape developed. In an effort to abort such attempts Virginia enacted the following statute:

> 1660, Act XXII. It is enacted that in case any English servant shall run away in company with any Negroes who are incapable of making satisfaction by addition of time that the English so running away shall serve for the time of the Negroes' absence as they are to do for their own by a former act.[14]

During the interim period between 1619 when blacks first arrived in Jamestown, Virginia, and 1660, when one of the first slave Acts was enacted, certain limited privileges and rights of blacks were recognized by the colonists. Examples of such recognition were: the court allowing a black servant, John Graweere, to purchase his child from a master upon the condition the child would be oriented in the Christian religion and a black servant being allowed to keep half of his benefit from raising hogs, so long as he surrendered the other half unto his master.[15]

Higginbotham documents how the courts and legislatures of the colonies gradually clarified the ambiguity of servitude and slavery, and how justice for white males over blacks and white females was defined by court-decided cases, and eventually by statutes. In the Sweat case decided by the Virginia Court in 1640, Robert Sweat (presumed white) fathered a child by a black woman servant of a master who was a military officer. The court ruled:

> [The] said negro woman shall be whipt at the whipping post and the said Sweat shall tomorrow in the forenoon do public penance for his offense at James city church in the time of devine service according to the laws of England in that the case provided.

Also in 1640, a black male named Emmanuel and four white servants stole "the skiff of Pierce, and corn, powder and shotguns," and conspired to escape. All having been convicted, the Virginia court required the Dutch leader of the group to wear shackles for one year, the second white servant to serve the colony for an extra seven years, the third white servant, "who was to be branded and whipped, was required to serve the colony for three years," and the fourth white servant, for two years. Emmanuel, who was black, "was whipped, branded with an 'R' in the cheek, and required to wear shackles for one year." Presumably, no additional time in service was required of Emmanuel because he was already deemed subjected to servitude for life.[16]

During the same year, three runaway servants, Victor and Gregory, white, and John Punch, black, were captured and convicted. All were sentenced to be whipped but the Court imposed additional and different sentences for the same crime:

> one called Victor, a dutchman, the other a Scotchman called James Gregory, shall first serve out their time with their master according to their Indentures, and one whole year apiece after the time of their service is Expired . . . and after that service . . . to serve the colony for three whole years apiece, and that the third being a negro named John Punch shall serve his said master or his assigns for the time of his natural life here or elsewhere.[17]

Further demonstrating injustice and the property nature in which blacks were perceived by the white colonists were the legal instruments (wills and contracts) by which blacks were sold or transferred from one master to another. In 1646, a black woman and her child were sold by Francis Potts to Stephen Carlton, providing, "to the use of him forever." A deed by William Wittington for the sale of a ten-year-old black girl provided in part, "along with any issue (children) she might produce for her and her children's lifetime and their successors forever." Such legal phraseology is descriptive of the same language used by lawyers in wills and contracts for the transfer of personal and real property. Other court decisions reveal how blacks prosecuted for committing the same offense as whites were more severely punished than white offenders. The above and many similar decisions by the Virginia colonial courts made it crystal clear that blacks were perceived as inferior, and the court's proclamations and enforcements were designed to assure the denigration of blacks to a status of subhuman beings.[18]

7

In 1639, probably out of fear of insurrection by blacks, the Virginia legislature joined hands with the courts in disarming blacks by enacting its first statute excluding blacks from the unrestricted access to purchase arms and ammunitions. From 1636 to 1680, other acts were enacted, increasing the term of service for non-indentured servants, and other acts were designed to assure the capture, retention, and the perpetuation of servitude of runaway black servants. As the slave population grew, so did such legislation in number and the severity of penalties for their violation.[19]

In 1662 Virginia further shaped the servitude of blacks towards slavery by enacting a law which provided that children born free or in bondage in the colony would hold the condition of the mother. Although another law in 1667 provided that slaves could be baptized as Christians, it also provided "the conferring of baptism doth not alter the condition of the person as to his bondage or freedom."[20]

To protect a master from punishment for killing a slave, the Virginia legislature enacted the following act in 1669:

An Act about the Casual killing of slaves.
Whereas the only law in force for the punishment of refractory servants resisting their master, mistress or overseer, cannot be inflicted on negroes [because the punishment was extension of time], Nor the obstinacy of many of them by other than violent means supprest. Be it enacted and declared by this grand assembly, if any slave resist his master . . . and by the extremity of the correction should chance to die, that his death shall not be accompted Felony, but the master (or that other person appointed by the master to punish him) be acquit from molestation, since it cannot be presumed that propensed malice (which alone makes murther Felony) should induce any man to destroy his own estate.

The above act of 1669 permitted masters and overseers to declare open season on their slaves, by beating, mutilating, or killing them to exact the maximum cooperation and work from them for the financial benefit of the masters' plantation.[21]

Further motivated by a combination of fear of insurrection, racial bias, and greed, Virginia enacted the first major slave code during 1680–1682, which became the model for black repression throughout colonial America. The act provided:

> 1680, Act X. Whereas the frequent meetings of considerable numbers of Negro slaves under pretense of feasts and burials is judged of dangerous consequence [it] enacted that no Negro or slave may carry arms, such as any club, staff, gun, sword, or other weapon, nor go from his owner's plantation without a certificate and then only on necessary occasions; the punishment twenty lashes on the bare back, well laid on. And further, if any Negro lift up his hand against any Christian he shall receive thirty lashes, and if he absent himself or lie out from his master's service and resist lawful apprehension, he may be killed and this law shall be published every six months.

Thus the Virginia legislators contemplated the freedom of locomotion of blacks would be essentially curtailed, the risk of blacks resisting slave control with any kind of weapon would be substantially reduced, and the potential threat of a black raising a hand against a Christian (white) for all practical purposes would be restrained. The Act of 1692 was enacted to remedy ineffectiveness of the 1680 Act by reinforcing it with wider publication of the provisions of both acts and by prohibiting any master or overseer from allowing any black slave to remain upon his plantation in excess of four hours without permission from the slave's master. Neither Act achieved the degree of effectiveness intended by the legislators.[22]

With these statutory clarifications the transition of Negroes from servitude to unmitigated slavery was complete.

Although the vast majority of blacks were relegated to a subservient status with limited social contact with free whites, other problems soon surfaced as a result of their presence and sexual intimacy with whites (especially black males).

E. Franklin Frazier noted that since the needs of the agrarian culture of the southern colonies demanded masculine labor, the early importations of slaves from Africa consisted mostly of able-bodied males. The result was a substantially disproportionate number of males over females in the slave population, which was not equalized until 1840. However, that disparity in the male-female population imposed a restraint upon the sexual expression of the male slaves which contributed to widespread sexual exploitation of the under-represented black females and probably also accounted for numerous cases of sexual activity between the black male slaves and indentured white women.[23]

It is also apparent that white concern about interracial sexual activity was further aggravated by a frequent result of such sexual relations—miscegenation.

Historically and currently miscegenation or biological mixing as a result of interracial marriage and sexual relations occurs wherever and whenever unlike ethnic groups meet and occupy the same area.[24] Participation in such interracial sexual or marital relations has been scorned and frowned upon by ethnic groups throughout history, but the cultural condemnation has never been sufficient to abate the practice. In fact, prohibitions against miscegenation—interracial marriage or interbreeding—have not had the success intended by efforts of ethnic groups to preclude the practice.

Lerone Bennett noted that according to historians James Hugo Johnston, Carter G. Woodson, and A. W. Calhoun, a considerable amount of miscegenation transpired between white indentured servants and black servants of both sexes, prior and subsequent to the arrival of blacks in 1619. Such relationships resulted in numerous mulatto children whose burden of support fell upon individual masters and society. During the initial years after 1619, most interracial sexual contact and marriages involved black men and white women. Such relations were not confined to servants, but often involved wives and other members of families of masters. However, with the advent of King Cotton and the plantation system, "the focus shifted from white women and Negro men to white men and Negro women . . . . "[25]

Plantation amalgamation, as a rule, was the result of what Calhoun called "the master's right of rape." And although mutual attraction played a part in some relationships, force or the threat of force defined all of the relationships. Despite what some commentators say, every sexual contact between a slaveholder and a slave woman was a symbolic or *de facto* rape, for the simple reason that the *institution* of slavery and the power of slaveholders destroyed the possibility of free choice. Another and related problem here was the indefensible position of a whole class of women whose only weapons were sexual ones. What all this boils down to is that the position of the slave woman was indefensible. And the fact that rape was a real and ever-present possibility was only a metaphor of the extreme vulnerability of her position.[26]

In white-male-dominated colonial America, the white population insisted on racial sexual integrity.[27] Insistence on white male racial integrity was not followed in practice nor equitably prohibited by legislation or enforced by court decree. Such insistence was evidently based, not only upon the visual racial and cultural distinction of blacks and the slave status to which they were relegated, but upon the frequent by-product of white-black sexual relations—interbreeding—amalgamated or hybrid offspring. Initially, the racial identity of such offspring (mulattos) had not been conclusively established by colonial society. Within their hybrid bodies, mulattos carried hereditary genes possessing dominant Negroid (black) and recessive Caucasoid (white) traits. Consequently, mulatto hybrids, or any of their offspring, could arrive in the world in unpredictable instances, visually identifiable with the Negroid (black) race, and in other instances, identifiable with the Caucasian race.

The skin color or racial visibility of the Negro slave aided slaveholders in perpetuating their status in bondage. Except in Delaware, anyone with black skin was presumed a slave and everyone with white skin was presumed a free person. This presumption made escape for black slaves more difficult because they were easily detected by the trademark of their skin, while the skin color of visually white indentured persons was not a badge of their status. For several years the offspring of a Negro slave father and a free white mother was free, while the offspring of a Negro slave mother and a free white father was a slave. However, an offspring of racially mixed parentage presented problems, depending upon the degree of their mixture and appearance. In 1849 the Virginia code provided that every person with one-fourth part or more Negro blood was a "mulatto" and a mulatto was a Negro. In other southern states the term "mulatto" was defined to include a "quadroon" (one fourth Negro), a person with one Negro grandparent, or an "octoroon" (one eighth Negro), a person with one Negro great grandparent. Meanwhile, South Carolina courts refused to rule that persons with any Negro blood were legally Negroes, but held instead that there must be a visible mixture to be declared a Negro, otherwise such persons were white.[28]

It may be reasonably inferred from the above biological distinctions that the efforts of legislatures and courts to racially define offsprings of mixed blood and the history of whites' insistence on racial sexual integrity—that early colonists had learned what geneticists later verified that dominant Negroid traits would prevail in visibility over recessive Caucasoid traits. With this realization and legislation enacted defining "race" and prohibiting interracial marriage or sexual relations, the early colonists must have shared the same fear and concern expressed by many whites years later—eventual annihilation of the white race by amalgamation. Consequently, colonial society racially classified such hybrid offspring as Negro, irrespective of their racial visibility.

Thus, the first statute clearly prohibiting miscegenation was enacted by Virginia legislature in 1691. It provided:

> Whatsoever English or other white man or woman, bond or free, shall intermarry with a Negro, Mulatto, or Indian man or woman, bond or free, he shall within 3 months be banished from this dominion forever . . . [29]
>
> White males were aware of the cultural condemnation as well as the legal and genetic consequences of miscegenation. Nevertheless, while they preached and insisted on racial integrity, a large number of them did not practice such loyalty when it came to interracial sexual activity. This fact is well substantiated by the numerous mulatto population present in Virginia in 1700 and thereafter. However, since leadership and control of colonial America were dominated by the ruling white male population, a dual standard of justice existed, ranging from exemption to various degrees of leniency for white males over white females and blacks who participated in interracial marriages or sexual relations in the order as follows: (1) white males; (2) white females; (3) black females; (4) black males.[30]

As Higginbotham stated:

> The legal process was tolerant of white male illicit "escapades" involving either white females or black females, but it was relatively

harsh on infractions by white females (even when involving white males) and brutally harsh on infractions between black males and white females.[31]

This bias in favor of white males as opposed to black males and white females is also manifest in the 1691 Miscegenation Act, which in part further provided: that any free English woman having a bastard child by a Negro shall pay fifteen pounds to the church wardens. In the event of default in payment, she would be disposed of for five years, with her prison earnings to be divided equally with the government, the parish and the informer. The statute was later amended to penalize a white male or female if either legitimized the relationship with the Negro in marriage, by banishing him or her from the colony forever. Strangely, no penalty was provided for the Negro partner or for a white man carrying on a clandestine relationship in which a black woman bore his bastard child. Thus, the possibility for pregnancy and the stern penalty for becoming impregnated by a black man significantly lessened the chances of a white woman becoming involved in a clandestine relationship with a black man.[32] Perhaps this dual standard of justice was the origin of the popular and exaggerated saying amongst blacks, "that only a white man and a black woman are free."

Higginbotham observes that this double standard of justice involving intra and interracial sexual activity was the result of . . . a socialization process of a white male dominated society; and that such interracial sexual activity was more sensitive and threatening to white male dominance, which provoked an interest exceeding the bounds of normal concerns about sexual relations.[33]

It was only after a white English woman had a bastard child by a black male did the law make such interracial conduct a crime for a black male and a white male alike. In 1705, the Virginia General Assembly clarified to some extent the status of offspring of black and white partners by providing that all mulatto children shall be servants at least until they are thirty-one years old. Since the penalty for legitimizing bastard relationships was ineffective in deterring the occurrence, the 1705 Act increased the penalty for such conduct as follows:

Whatsoever white man or woman being free shall intermarry with a Negro shall be committed to prison for 6 months without bail, and pay 10 pounds to the use of the parish. Ministers marrying such persons shall pay 10 thousand pounds of tobacco.[34]

Again, strangely, no imprisonment penalty was imposed for blacks but the imprisonment penalty for whites was increased from six to twelve months in 1848. Notwithstanding, it was not until 1932 that the statute was amended to impose a penalty of imprisonment for whites and blacks intermarrying. The penalty was thereafter increased to confinement in the penitentiary from one to five years. The courts on occasion granted a divorce or annulled a marriage when there was evidence that a white female had sexual relations with a slave or free black male. No such marital dissolution was proclaimed when the evidence showed a black female had sexual relations with a white male. These earlier and sterner measures did not minimize or preclude interracial sexual conduct.[35]

As Higginbotham states:

With these rigid statutory restrictions written by white males, one might think that interracial sexual relationships during the colonial period would have become nonexistent. Instead, the statutes merely eliminated legitimation of marriages and encouraged the extensive exploitation of black women by their masters and other white men, thus explaining the presence of thousands of mulattos in Virginia. The result was that there was probably more intermixture in the 1700s than since then. Despite moral taboos and criminal sanctions, "white men of every social rank slept with negro women. The Colonists as well as European travelers in the colonies frequently pointed to this fact of American life." Where interracial sex relations were involved, the legal system was operationally effective to the extent that white men maximized their options, dehumanized blacks,—white women and themselves.[36]

Other colonies enacted statutes against miscegenation and as late as 1951, twenty-nine northern and southern states had legislation prohibiting interracial marriage between whites and blacks, and thirteen states prohibited marriage between whites and other minorities of Mongolian blood.[37]

Sixteen states had such legislation in 1967 when the Supreme

Court declared them unconstitutional. The penalties for violating miscegenation statutes of the respective states varied in fines up to two thousand dollars and for imprisonment from a few months to ten years. Enforcement of such legislation presented numerous problems for the courts in interpreting *race* as defined by the statutes. Example: Georgia had a statute forbidding the marriage of any white to any person with "any ascertainable trace" of "African, West Indian, Asiatic Indian, or Mongolian blood." Some state statutes merely said "with any person of African descent," while others specified precise fractions ("one-fourth, one-eighth, one-sixteenth"),[38] or as Louisiana law for non-marriage purpose in 1983 says "one-thirty-second."

It is now clear that since colonial times, both races have known and understood how provocatively sensitive an issue interracial marriage, or intimate or heterosexual relations between black and white partners presented. However, no two sex members in each race (white-black) were more cognizant of that provocative sensitivity than a black male and a white female. For the penalty borne by a white female for such intimacy was unduly harsh, often involving family disinheritance, extreme community ostracism, as well as being an outcast as far as an opportunity for marriage by a white male was concerned. This was true even though the white female's white male partner might have been guilty of interracial sexual activity with a black female; for a black male, it was the forever unforgivable offense, with the almost certainty of him being brutally beaten, castrated or otherwise maimed, if not lynched. Perhaps it was for these known reasons that author Lillian Smith titled her book about such interracial intimacy, *Strange Fruit*[39] and why noted psychiatrist Alvin F. Poussaint characterizes such interracial intimacy as "forbidden fruit."[40] Evidence of the significance placed upon this sensitive sexual conduct will be seen as a contributing factor to the problems in white-black relations discussed in subsequent chapters. However, in view of this enlightening history of miscegenation, the hostility which it produced as well as the underlying colonial reasons for prohibiting the practice, one, as a matter of hindsight, will clearly see that the miscegenation statutes were but a forerunner of the segregation laws requiring separation of the races which became universal in the south two centuries later.

Notes

1. John Hope Franklin, *From Slavery to Freedom*, 5th ed. (New York: Alfred A. Knopf, Inc., 1980), 30–31.

2. Ibid., 36–39.

3. Ibid., 40–42.

4. Ibid., 41.

5. Ibid., 42–49.

6. A. Leon Higginbotham, Jr., *In the Matter of Color* (New York: Oxford University Press, 1978), 20.

7. Carter G. Woodson, *The Negro in Our History* (Washington, D.C.: Associated Publishers, Inc., 1972), 82–83. Franklin, 54.

8. Ibid., 84–85.

9. *The World Book Encyclopedia*, 1976 ed., s.v., "conditions of slavery," 416a.

10. Higginbotham, *In the Matter of Color*, 19.

11. Kenneth M. Stampp, *The Peculiar Institution, Slavery in the Antebellum South* (New York: Alfred A. Knopf, Inc., 1956), 18.

12. Ibid., 26.

13. Ibid., 24. For further reference see Richard Brandon Morris, *Government and Labor in Early America* (New York: Columbia University Press, 1946), 36–37, and Ulrich B. Phillips, *American Negro Slavery* (New York: D. Appleton and Company, 1918), 74–75, 87.

14. Higginbotham, *In the Matter of Color*, 34–37.

15. Ibid., 24–25.

16. Ibid., 27. H. R. McIlwaine, ed., *Minutes of the Council General Court of Colonial Virginia 1622–1632, 1670–1676* (Richmond, Virginia: Colonial Press, 1924), 467.

17. Higginbotham, 28. *In the Matter of Color* McIlwaine, ed., *Minutes of the Council General Court*, 466.

18. Higginbotham, *In the Matter of Color*, 26.

19. Ibid., 34–35.

20. Franklin, *From Slavery to Freedom*, 55.

21. Higginbotham, *In the Matter of Color*, 36. Henning, *Statutes*, 270.

22. Ibid., 39–40, 50 Guild, *Black Laws*, Act X, 45.

23. E. Franklin Frazier, *The Negro Family in the United States* (Chicago: University of Chicago Press, 1973), 17.

24. Brewton Berry, *Race Relations* (Boston: Houghton Mifflin Company, 1951), 247.

25. Lerone Bennett, Jr., *Before the Mayflower: A History of the Negro in America*, rev. ed. (Chicago: Johnson Publishing Company, 1964), 241–43.

26. Reprinted by permission of Lerone Bennett, Jr., *Before the Mayflower: A History of the Negro in America*, Fifth Edition 1961, 1982 (Johnson Publishing Company, Inc.), 307–308.

27. Higginbotham, *In the Matter of Color*, 40–41.

28. Stampp, *The Peculiar Institution*, 193–95.

29. Higginbotham, *In the Matter of Color*, 44.

30. Ibid., 40.

31. Ibid., 40–41.

32. Ibid., 44–45.

33. Ibid., 41.

34. Ibid., 46. See also Henning, *Statutes*, vol. 3, 453–54.

35. Ibid., 46–47.

36. Ibid., 46–47.

37. Berry, *Race Relations*, 253.

38. Ibid., 253.

39. Lillian Smith, *Strange Fruit* (New York: Harcourt Brace Jovanovich, 1944).

40. Alvin F. Poussaint, "The Black Male-White Female," *Ebony* Magazine, August 1983, 124–26.

Two Black Chattels

Chattel slavery, as distinguished from "servitude," is recognized by historians as the change in the form of slavery from servitude to the unqualified legal ownership of human beings for the exclusive purpose of performing labor and satisfying the general whim and caprice of the master-owner, essentially without financial compensation. This change occurred after passage of Act XXII by the Virginia Legislature in 1680, and similar slave codes subsequently enacted by the legislatures of several other slave colonies. As the slave population increased in the colonies by importation and human reproduction, so did colonial legislation to further obliterate any semblance of servitude and prevent an early emancipation of blacks. The legislative effect of the codes assured the complete dehumanization of blacks and relegated them to the state of "chattel"—an article of personal property such as a gun or tool, but perhaps more comparable to the slave, a mule, pig, or other species of livestock. So the duration of black servitude legally existed for only about forty-one years, from 1619 to 1660, followed by perpetual bondage (slavery) for twenty years, from 1660 to 1680, when chattel slavery was legally implemented.

The chattel character of slaves was enhanced further by the growth and development of commercial transactions and the efforts of colony legislatures to raise revenue. Consequently, some colonies levied a special tax on slaves as was levied on other property. Slaveowners sold slaves on credit, leased them to work for others, used them as collateral or security for credit, and sold them to satisfy the creditors of the deceased or legatees of an estate. In such transactions family ties were generally ignored although sometimes families were put up for sale as a unit. Slaves were also sold in auctions, awarded as prizes in lotteries and raffles, and wagered at gambling tables. Some slaves were given to white children as a present by affluent parents and many were devised by "will."[1]

Additional Virginia legislation in 1699 prohibited *manumission*—the act of freeing a slave by grant or will—by imposing upon a master committing the act, the obligation to provide transportation out of the country within six months for any freed black or mulatto. Since most masters could not afford such a financial undertaking, the bondage of blacks was thereby rendered perpetual.[2] By the eighteenth century skin color had become not only evidence of enslavement, but also a badge of degradation.[3]

Slavery, often referred to by authorities on the subject as the *peculiar institution,* must as a matter of intellectual curiosity, arouse questions in the mind of any normal human being as to why it was established, how it operated, and how and why did it endure for over two hundred years. It should first be recognized however, that slavery was largely an agricultural system of labor, shaped by the economic needs and desires of slaveowners and their personal ambition to escape the hard work involved in agricultural production, carried on largely in the hot climate of the southern United States.

The system consisted of small farms of as few as one, two, or four slaves with whom the master sometimes worked side-by-side to units with ten to thirty slaves having a definite but limited division of labor. Units with more than thirty slaves generally had a high degree of specialized labor, such as household servants, tool custodians, plow and hoe gangs, carpenters, blacksmiths, and caretakers of livestock. Ordinarily, slave units were not larger than one hundred because the larger the unit, the more difficult their management, although there were a few units as large as seven hundred.[4] This, however, does not mean that every white family owned slaves. As late as 1860, there were 8 million whites in the south and institutionalized slavery had a dominant influence on the economic thinking of the community. Nevertheless, as indigenous as slavery was ingrained in the culture, three-fourths of the white population neither owned slaves nor had immediate economic interest in maintaining the institution itself. This does not, however, alter the fact that the large plantations exerted the greater influence on the society.[5]

Large slave plantation units usually hired an overseer or foreman, often called a slavedriver, who in some instances worked, but in all instances, urged the gangs to work by verbal order or the use of a whip. The overseer's job was to maintain order and steady work, impose discipline, and get the slave gangs out an hour before daylight by ringing a bell or blowing a horn. He kept recorded inventory on the volume of work performed from what was called "day clean to first dark" (daylight to dusk) and made a bed-check of each slave cabin at night to assure the presence of each slave and to prevent any escape.[6]

The agricultural products of the system varied to some degree with the geographical location of slave colonies. The farm products of what is now the southeastern United States consisted largely of cotton, rice, tobacco, indigo, and sugar in the deep south (Louisiana). Hemp and other diversified products were cultivated in Kentucky and Missouri. Since agricultural products are essentially seasonal, slaveowners so organized the system to assure that different and necessary kinds of slave work were available for all four seasons of the year. There was no leisure time except half-day Saturday and all day Sunday. Indoor tasks were reserved for inclement weather. Masters either planned enough to provide for their slaves and livestock, or they allotted the slaves a small plot of land on which to plant for their own sustenance.

In order to achieve a profitable agricultural yield, slave-masters utilized slave labor under either the "Gang System"—where slaves worked under the command of a slavedriver who worked them at a daily fast pace, or the "Task System," where each hand was given a specific daily task. Slaves were also classified according to their ability and experience to perform various tasks essential to the labor system. Children were labeled "quarter hands," who advanced with physical maturity to "half hands," "three quarter hands," and "full hands" at eighteen years of age. Interestingly, the master rather than the parent decided at what age children would be put to work. They generally started as water toters or apprentices in the field with their mothers at ten or twelve years of age.[7] Aged or disabled slaves performed other non-field work. Elderly women cooked, sewed, laundered clothing, cared for small children, and did spinning and weaving.

Domestic servants were considered a prized vanity because the work was essentially light and clean. They worked as hostelers, coachmen, butlers, housemaids, cooks, footmen, laundresses, chambermaids, children's nurses, and personal servants. Personal

20

historical accounts of slaves reported by Frazier reveal how the position of "house servants" became a favored position of slaves because it meant better food, opportunity to listen to conversations of the master family, and learning many things, including the articulation of the English language, politeness, and gentility. House servants were sometimes envied and sometimes hated because they belonged to a privileged class which represented the most fundamental social distinction in status between field hands and themselves. The extent to which servants assimilated the language of whites and adopted their habits and attitudes depended upon the degree of intimacy between the master family and the slaves. The relationship of some masters with their slaves was quite humane, sometimes to the extent that masters supervised slaves in their general deportment, religion, sexual behavior, and marriage.[8]

Bondsmen were a select group of slave craftsmen who were exempted from field work because of their craft. They included engineers, carpenters, bricklayers, blacksmiths, stone masons, shoemakers, weavers, millers, and landscapers. Exceptionally talented bondsmen were sometimes hired out (leased) by their masters, and sometimes were hired out largely for their own benefit. The hirer was usually obligated by contract to keep the bondsmen well clothed. Hiring out of slaves was often done by executors of estates while the estate was being processed through administration. Husbands and children were also often hired out by urban masters.[9]

Quantity of Labor

The extent to which slaves were worked depended upon the sensitivity of the master and the size of the profits he desired. Some slaves were overworked and some were not, but most were worked excessively. During the harvest seasons slaves worked fifteen to sixteen hours a day, including time for meals and rest periods. Owners of large plantations were more susceptible to the hard driving which resulted in overworked slaves. While it is said that the majority of slaveowners did not sanction overworking slaves, most of them tolerated excessively heavier labor routines than they may have realized. As Stampp observed, "the records of plantation regime clearly indicate that slaves were more frequently overworked by calloused tyrants than overindulged by mellowed patriarchs." Some bondsmen suffered physical breakdown and early deaths from overwork. Most slaves were driven by overseers who were often selected on the basis of which overseer could produce the most yield and were often employed on a piece-work pay scale, as noted

> "It is too commonly the case that masters look only to the yearly products of their farms, and praise or condemn their overseers by this standard alone . . . . " This being the case, it was understandably of no consequence to the overseer that the old hands were "worked down" and the young ones "overstrained" that the "breeding women" miscarried, and that the "suckler" lost their children. "So that he has the requisite number of cotton bags, all is overlooked; he is re-employed at an advanced salary, and his reputation increased."[10]

In keeping with the practice of maximum use of daylight for labor "day clean to first dark," an ex-slave remembered "seeing slave women hurrying to their work in early morning with their shoes and stockings in their hands, and a petticoat wrapped over their shoulders to dress in the field the best way they could."[11]

An ardent defender of slavery describing a group of planters he called "Cotton Snobs" or "Southern Yankees" wrote that in their frantic quest for wealth "the crack of the whip was heard early and late, until their bondsmen were bowed to the ground with over-tasking and over-toil."[12] Excessive labor in the heat of mid-summer inevitably took its toll on slaves who could not bear the hard driving and without noon rest, collapsed in the fields. A Mississippi planter reported "numerous cases of sunstroke," and in Virginia it was reported that hot weather and heavy labor caused "the death of many Negroes in the harvest fields."[13]

Perpetual Control of Slaves

Wise and bright-eyed youngsters of today often ask how did slave masters manage to keep so many slaves in bondage for so many generations. Their innocent but logical curiosity is quickly laid to rest, however, once they are acquainted with the various and less familiar techniques of slave control other than physical restriction by chains and imprisonment or the use of violence against slaves. Some slave control-measures are described in detail by Stampp.

One of the cardinal rules of slave management was to establish and maintain strict discipline. The slave was made to understand that "the master was to govern absolutely and the slave was to obey implicitly."[11] The master was to implant in the mind and spirit of the slaves themselves a consciousness of inferiority that they had "to know and keep their place . . . to understand that bondage was their natural status . . . " and that their African ancestry, their color was a badge of degradation. The slaves were to display respect and never disrespect any white person, to give the right-of-way to whites on the streets, and never to become familiar or intimate with whites. The essence of every state's slave code required slaves "to submit to their masters and respect all white men."[14]

As a North Carolina judge once wrote:

Any number of acts . . . may constitute "insolence"—it may be merely a look, the pointing of a finger, a refusal or neglect to step out of the way when a white person is seen to approach. But each of such acts violates the rules of propriety, and if tolerated, would destroy that subordination, upon which our social system rests.[15]

A master must instill in slaves "fear of the power of the master . . . " and "[M]ake them stand in fear." Fear was accomplished with the slave's knowledge of the master's authority, further manifested by a peculiar tone of voice or the display or use of a whip. Masters were to impress their slaves with their own helplessness, creating in them a psychological consciousness of dependency upon the master for their existence and subsistence.

While all of these objectives were seldom achieved, each master knew the average slave was an imperfect copy of the model and was never to be trusted.[16] It should be interesting to note how long after slavery a semblance of these techniques of psychological brainwashing persisted in modified form into and through the period of legal segregation as will be later seen in the chapter on segregation.

In order to implement the above objectives of control, a set of master's rules was established with which overseers were to comply. Some of such rules are described by Stampp as follows:

a. The overseer was never to be absent from the fields while the slaves were at work and he was to search their cabins for stolen goods and weapons and guard the keys to the smokehouse, corn crib, and stable.

b. Slaves were not to be out of their cabin after "horn blow" (generally 8 P.M. in the winter and 9 P.M. in the summer), and night watches were scheduled for masters and overseers to check the cabins to account for every slave.

c. Slaves were not to leave the estate without a pass indicating their destination and time of return.

d. Whites and free Negroes were not to work with slaves and slave contact with strangers or persons from other plantations was restricted.

e. Slaves were often required to select their spouses from among other slaves of the master on the plantation, although sometimes a master purchased a spouse for his slave from another plantation to retain smooth control over the bride and groom. Otherwise, the couple would have to remain single.

f. Masters often used the divide-and-control technique by selecting slaves they thought would be loyal and supportive of the master, as opposed to loyalty to the slaves. Usually they were domestics, headdrivers, skilled artists and foremen, who were encouraged to remain aloof and feel superior to field hands. They were rewarded with special privileges—better clothes and more food. They were often instrumental in assisting the master to capture runaway slaves. If found disloyal to the master they were demoted to a field hand.

g. The penalty for attempted escape was to be sold away from family and friends to slave owners in the deep south—the Georgia swamps or the Louisiana sugar district, where slave life was deemed more severe and the possibility of escape more difficult.

h. After colonial legislatures repealed Christian baptism as a qualification for freedom, slaveholders believed Christian indoctrination would benefit the slaves in their moral relations, induce them to become more honest and faithful servants, and help to keep them docile and contented. Other slaveholders believed it was a dangerous practice because of mischief resulting from religious meetings.

i. Some slaveholders gave their slaves a plot of land on which to cultivate crops for themselves, or paid them a few dollars to inspire them to toil without rebellion.[17.]

Other Measures of Control

Prior to 1850 slaves were branded and mutilated, and male slaves were sometimes castrated, but these earlier tortures were seldom performed thereafter. To prevent slaves from escaping, they were tracked with dogs called "Negro dogs," trained to track slaves. Some slaveholders permitted their "Negro dogs" to give their victims a severe mauling as a lesson to deter future efforts to escape.[18]

Physical locomotion of a slave was restricted and he had to present a "pass" when demanded by any white man. Forging a pass or free papers by a slave was a felony. The congregation of more than five slaves for any purpose, in the absence of a white person, irrespective of how orderly, constituted unlawful assembly.

Slaves were not permitted to beat drums or blow horns, or to possess or purchase guns or liquor without written permission from the master. Ironically, while they prepared food, served it, and cared for the master family, they were not permitted to administer medicine to whites or practice medicine.

Neither a slave nor white person was permitted to teach a slave to read, write, or set type in a printing office, or to give him or her books or pamphlets. Many slaves nevertheless learned to read.

It was unlawful for any person to trade with slaves or sell them liquor without permission or to give them a "pass," gamble with them (probably for fear they might win a huge sum of money and escape), to teach them to read or write, or to write or utter anti-slavery material. The penalty for doing so was severe.

The penalty was death for anyone to conceal a slave, aid his escape, or encourage bondsmen to rebel. Every state had slave patrols consisting of slaveholders under a certain age (Alabama, slaveholders sixty and non-slaveholders forty-five years) to perform patrol duty one night a week to prevent insurrection.[19]

Punishment

Punishment was the primary measure of slave control because colonial society and slaveholders learned early that slaves did not submit willingly to slavery but had to be persuaded with favorable rewards or punishment, the authority of which was conferred upon the master by state law. All other means of control were secondary to punishment.

Forms of punishment described by Stampp were as follows:

1. Demotion from domestic, foreman, or driver to field hand.
2. Denial of passes to incorrigible slaves.
3. Forbidding slaves from participating in Saturday night dances.
4. Forcing malingerers to work on Sundays and holidays.
5. Confiscating the crop from their "truck patches."
6. Reducing the sum of value due them.
7. Selling them away from family and loved ones.
8. Giving male field hands women's work (laundering, cooking, et cetera).
9. Jailing them on the premises.
10. Jailing them in the public jail for a fee.
11. Confinement in the stockades.
12. Rationing their meals.
13. Enshackling the ankle with a chain and ball or the neck with an iron collar.
14. The whip was the most common means of punishment (the emblem of the Master's authority). Many masters believed flogging should not be inflicted in anger since the certainty rather than the severity of the procedure was what made it effective. From fifteen to twenty lashes were common, and as many as 100 for maximum punishment. The whip was usually made of rawhide because it lacerated the skin.

Insurrection or serious crimes committed by slaves acting in concert probably provoked the most barbaric of all reactions by white slaveholders. The fear of rebellion provoked by such slave conduct resulted in angry mob action described by a Louisiana mistress as "Lintch's Law," which involved breaking into homes or jails, apprehending the accused, and without a legitimate inquest or court trial, burning, or perhaps most often, hanging them from a tree. As Stampp describes:

> Mobs all too frequently dealt with slaves accused of murder or rape . . . They conducted their own trials or broke into jails or courtrooms to seize prisoners for summary execution. Their most fortunate victims were hanged; the others were burned to death, sometimes in the presence of hundreds of bondsmen who were forced to attend the ceremony.[20]

While there were no legally established requirements for slave ownership and brutality was more prevalent on the large plantations, some state laws required slaveholders to be humane to slaves by furnishing them with adequate food and clothing and providing them with proper care in sickness and old age.[21]

Thus it is clear that slaves were viewed and treated as personal property in a manner akin to livestock, which had to be nurtured and cared for in the interest of their subsistence for the financial profitability of their master. Individual masters, depending upon their moral attitude, struggled with the dilemma of this contradiction called "human property," in knowing and deciding where the line of the property character ended, and the line of human character began.

Attitudes of Slaves and Masters toward Bondage

With such diverse measures of slave control one must necessarily wonder what was the attitude of slaves towards their bondage and how did their white masters interpret their attitude. Contrary to the assertions of some authors that the slaves were quite contented and submitted rather willingly to the regime, historical evidence demonstrates that they felt the burden of the system mostly in their lack of control over their own time and labor. Their apparent acquiescence was deceptive. When they yielded to the powerful authority of the master, they generally did so because they saw no other practical choice. Evidence of this state of mind is the abundance of data revealing the dilemma posed for those holding and maintaining slaves.

Many masters acknowledged they had considerable trouble as slaveholders because slaves were what they called "troublesome property." Resistance by slaves posed an ever present problem of discipline and most of them, at some time or another, expressed their discontent by protesting about some aspects of the system. Many of them yearned to be free, although as they grew older, hope and spirit faded. Some, however, never abandoned hope or stopped resisting. They were characterized by slavelords as:

> The "bad character" of this "insolent, surly and unruly" sort made them a liability to those who owned them, for a slave's value was measured by his disposition as much as by his strength and skills. Such rebels seldom won legal freedom, yet they never quite admitted they were slaves.[22]

Many slaves manifested dual impulses toward their masters and their duties. Sometimes they appeared to derive personal satisfaction from doing a job well, and at other times, they showed a propensity to resist authority or outwit their masters by doing a poor job or none at all. Which impulse prevailed depended upon a given time. Perhaps one of the enigmatic observations of a rational and just person reading about the reactions of masters to the attitude of slaves toward their own bondage is the very contradiction in "human property" itself. Many masters reacted as though they could not understand why their slaves did not appreciate their status, even though the system went against the grain of human nature for man to be free, or at least, not enslaved.

Masters were constantly confounded in their efforts to psyche themselves into believing or pretending they understood their slaves on the one hand, and utterly frustrated by the slaves' inconsistent unwillingness and rebellion on the other. As a former slave described:

> . . . The bondsmen had good reason for encouraging their master to underrate their intelligence. Ignorance was a "high virtue in a human chattel," he suggested, and since it was the master's pur-

pose to keep his bondsmen in this state, they were shrewd enough to make him think he succeeded. A Virginia planter concluded from his long experience that many slaveholders were victimized by the "sagacity" of Negroes whom they mistakenly thought they understood so well. He was convinced that the slaves, "under the cloak of great stupidity," made "dupes" of their masters. The most general defect in the character of the Negro, is hypocrisy: and this hypocrisy frequently makes him pretend to more ignorance than he possesses; and if his master treats him as a fool, he will be sure to act the fool's part. This is a very convenient trait, as it frequently serves as an apology for awkwardness and neglect of duty."[23]

Masters knew that slaves would not work when they could get away with it, and that they would not perform any more work than they had to. While such attitudes can be clearly understood as ways of expressing resentment, and as techniques of surviving overwork or death, masters called such slaves "slow," "lazy," "an eye servant," or "trifling negroes." However, few slaves seemed ashamed of such descriptions or appellations.

Many masters learned that any attempt to force slaves beyond the work limits they set for themselves would only result in diminishing returns, rendering the crop yield unprofitable. Besides slowing down work, many slaves bedeviled their master by performing careless work or damaging property, partly out of irresponsibility and partly out of intentional and deliberate mischief. A Louisiana physician, Samuel W. Cartwright, in search of a "rationalization" for such attitudes or conduct, attributed such work habits to a disease peculiar to Negroes which he called "Dysathesia Ethiopia"—one who did much mischief that appeared intentional. Often the mischief would involve damaging tools and crops or abusing livestock. Other slaveholders in search of an explanation or more appropriately, a rationalization for such conduct called it "Rascality." Dr. Cartwright ridiculously rationalized further that the propensity of slaves to run away was due to a disease of the mind which he called "Draptomania." This disease he contended could be cured with proper medical advice.[24] While Dr. Cartwright did not describe the medical advice, one might think that any rational and objective person would have concluded that the only cure was a dose of permanent freedom.

Slaveholding—Economic Security and Mental Insecurity

Additional evidence that slaveholding was no bed of roses was the ongoing relationship between the master and his slaves. It was mostly a contest of wills, with the master often being outwitted by the slaves who frequently knew him better then he knew them. Slaves resorted to various schemes to avoid work and rebel against the oppression of their bondage. Some of such designs were malingering—contriving illnesses, engaging in work slowdown, fomenting trouble between the master and the overseer by frequently complaining to the master in an effort to cause him to dismiss the overseer;[25] "slave sabotage"—inflicting injury (mayhem or illnesses) upon themselves such as throwing a shoulder out of place, inserting an arm in a beehive, drinking a mildly harmful medication to cause illness, or even cutting off a finger or hand to avoid being sold to a distant location. Some newly imported slaves resisted enslavement to the extreme measure of committing suicide by hanging or drowning themselves. Some runaway slaves resisted their recapture by killing their pursuers or killing themselves.[26]

Slave Fugitives

Slaves have attempted escape to freedom since they were first brought to this continent in 1619. When slaves ran away newspaper advertisements for runaway slaves often amusingly stated that they ran away for no reason. However, the most common reason for slaves running away was being separated from their families by a master's arbitrary sale of a family member. Other reasons for running away were to escape heavy or excessive work, to avoid punishment (having been severely whipped), and the general resentment of slavery. In making their getaway, slaves often helped themselves to the master's money or goods to facilitate their escape. Sometimes other slaves gave refuge by providing food, clothes, or temporary shelter, or by writing a "pass" for them, for their travel mostly by night and sleep-by-day adventure.

Runaways took anything that was not secured by lock and key and they were described by slaveholders as inherently dishonest. The slaves, however, made a distinction between "stealing" and "taking." When they appropriated things from the master, it was taking a part of his master's bounty for another part of his bounty (slaves).[27]

Slaves Were Not Always Humble

The escape of slaves was a high risk one because they were easily identifiable by their non-white appearance and their general illiteracy and limited knowledge of geography. Augmenting these difficulties was the fact that all white men were legally authorized to seize and return runaway slaves. Some white men became professional bounty hunters for rewards offered by slaveowners.[28] Most of the slaves who attempted escape and most of those who were successful came from the upper south, where distance to free territories was considerably shorter.[29] Most fugitives knew that failure in their attempted escape meant they would be sold away from their families to the deep south.[30]

In approximately 1803, slave fugitives were also encouraged and assisted in their escape by white abolitionists primarily from the north. Abolitionists were Quakers and other religious groups, including some free blacks who strongly disapproved of slavery. Thus, the combined assistance to fugitive slaves rendered largely by slaves not venturing escape and northern abolitionists became known as the underground railroad. It was so named because of the rapid, secret, and almost mysterious methods of slave escape which left slaveowners and hunters baffled.

Usually the routes of slave escape north were through Pennsylvania and Ohio into northern states and Canada. Later opportunities of escape were made available through other northern states. However, northern laws against fugitive slaves were enacted as early as 1648 in New York, providing a penalty of 150 fl. for any person harboring or giving aid or comfort to slave fugitives.[31] Reinforcing state laws, Congress enacted laws in 1793 and again, as part of the compromise of 1850, providing for the surrender and deportation of slaves who successfully gained freedom by having fled into free territories.

Some slaves who escaped to freedom joined the underground railroad movement to help other slaves escape. One such person was Harriet Tubman, who herself had been enslaved twenty-five years and eluded her bondage in Maryland. Another was Josiah Henson, who also escaped from his master in Maryland. Between 1850 and 1859, Tubman returned to the south nineteen times and delivered several hundred fugitive slaves to freedom. Aggrieved slaveowners offered $40,000 for her capture, but Tubman and Henson continued to conduct fugitives to freedom by using numerous routes through Kentucky and Tennessee to Canada.[32]

There was also Connecticut-born John Brown, who grew up in Ohio detesting slavery and became a radical abolitionist. He helped slaves to escape by underground and violent measures. After capturing the arsenal at Harpers Ferry in October 1859, he was captured and hanged December 2 of the same year.

From southern record evidence, Phillips wrote of numerous killings of masters and other whites by the hands of slaves. Slaveholders kept slaves whom they feared were capable of murdering them or burning down their dwelling at night. While being punished, one domestic slave turned upon her mistress, threw her down, and beat her unmercifully about the head and face. Another body servant of a humane master who rarely punished his slaves, "waylaid his owner, knocked him down with a white oak club and beat his head to a pumice." Such occurrences made it appear foolish to place confidence in slaves. Although slave violence sometimes erupted for no apparent reason, the most common provocation was an attempt by a master or overseer to work or punish a slave severely. The boldest as well as the most contented appearing slave at times resorted to violence, and the usual consequence was death for the slave.[33]

Slave Rebellion

Slaves continually plotted rebellion against slavery, often putting the white population in a state of fear of considerable proportions. One of such plots of insurrection was led by Denmark Vesey of Charleston, South Carolina. Vesey was a "free black" since 1800 who lived a comfortable life but was disenchanted with his freedom and the continued enslavement of other blacks. He carefully selected his leaders and they collected weapons— bayonets, daggers and pikeheads—over a number of years. The revolt was scheduled to take place on the second Sunday in July 1822, but whites were informed and Vesey advanced the date thirty days. However, word of the change did not reach all of his men and the insurrection was swiftly quelled. Vesey and 138 others were arrested, of whom 42 were condemned.[34]

Many high school students have read about the insurrection of Nat Turner in Southhampton County, Virginia. On August 22, 1831, Turner, joined by about seventy other slaves, killed his master's family and about sixty whites. Turner was reputed to be a pious man, as humble and docile as a slave was expected to be, and manifested no evidence of being overworked or underfed. Members of his band said they had suffered enough punishment. The rebellion was quickly quelled within forty-eight hours by the mobilization of whites in overwhelming strength. During the massacre which followed, many innocent slaves were slaughtered and Turner was arrested two months later (October 30). He was convicted November 5 and hanged November 11, 1831. Many members of his band were slaughtered while others were transported to distant locations.

However, the Turner rebellion and the thought of a similar recurrence left slaveholders apprehensive three decades later. Strangely, white slaveholders viewed slave violence as acts of ingratitude. When no real violence was in progress, rumors of violence circulated in southern communities, perpetuating the sleepless apprehension of whites of slave insurrection. Correspondingly, the speed with which Turner's insurrection was aborted and the bloody massacre which followed it served as a restraining reminder to slaves of the risk involved in violent rebellion.[35] These fears, although varying in degree, remained a part of the institution of slavery for its duration.

Impact of Slavery on the Slave Family

Perhaps one of the most painful and irreparably damaging effects on the family of slaves was the right and practice of the master to sell its members. How many viable slave families were disorganized or destroyed as a result of separation of their members by sale can never be known. It is practically impossible to comprehend the emotional and psychological impact the sale of children had upon parents and other siblings left behind. The sale of one parent from spouse and children must have left unimaginable emotional and economic consequences for the remaining members. When the husband-father was sold, a mother was undoubtedly faced with the awesome responsibility of child rearing, not to mention the task of trying to reconcile field labor with motherhood. These dual responsibilities, often assumed by slave mothers in the absence of a father, gave rise to a dominating position of the mother in the family, which Frazier attributes to the origin of the matriarch, or the matrifocal influence of the mother in many black families.

Although women often had the added ordeal of forced cohabitation, seldom were they ever spared the rigors of the daily routine, as E. Franklin Frazier cites from the personal account of Moses Grandy, an ex-slave:

> On the estate I am speaking of, those women who had sucking children suffered much from their breasts becoming full of milk, the infant being left at home; they therefore could not keep up with the other hands; I have seen the overseer beat them with raw hide, so that the blood and milk flew mingled from their breasts. A woman who gives offence in the field, and is large in the family way, is compelled to lie down over a hole made to receive her corpulency and is flogged with the whip, or beat with a paddle, which had holes in it; at every stroke comes a blister. One of my sisters was so severely punished in this way, that labor was brought on, and the child was born in the field. This very overseer, Mr. Brooks, killed in this manner a girl named Mary; her father and mother were in the field at the time.[36]

Even when mothers delivered full-term babies they were often ordered back to labor in the field three or four weeks after birth, carrying their infant with them to be left alone in the shade, or cared for by a child. If a slave mother were a domestic servant to the master family, she was often obligated to give priority in care to the infant of her mistress over her own. This demand sometimes resulted in the slave mother developing a stronger attachment for the child of the mistress than she held for her own. However, this was not always the case, since many slave mothers developed a deep and lasting sentiment for their own children, which was manifested with the children in the cabin, of which she was the mistress.

The impact to which the maternal feelings of slave mothers were affected by their circumstances cannot be determined, but it is clear many of them endured great suffering in their efforts to see their children when they were separated by miles. As Frazier noted, such separation of children from parents was characterized by Washington Irving as "a peculiar evil of slavery." Compounding the rigorous labor routines of pregnant slave women was the high rate of miscarriages. It was not uncommon for a female slave to experience two, three or five miscarriages, if not more.[37]

Further compounding a generally already complicated and ruptured slave-family organization was the mulatto by-product of those amorous and promiscuous unions between free whites and Negro slaves. Not only were mulatto slaves often accorded preferential treatment by their kinfolk in the master class, but the female mulatto was frequently a preferred commodity by the male members of the master group. Often endowed with the physical attributes more in concurrence with Caucasian physical characteristics, she was frequently selected for domestic service. A few masters paid premium prices for her to become his mistress, kept woman, or sometimes for prostitution of a private and permanent nature. When the latter arrangement developed, it represented an almost "socially approved system of concubinage" which was found in Charleston, Mobile, and New Orleans.[38]

In some situations the sexual intimacy between white men and slave women was based upon genuine sentiment, with the slave woman satisfying a polygamous role as a second wife, without religious or legal sanction. In this capacity the slave paramour was often the rival of her white mistress. Moreover, she and her mulatto offspring were sometimes rewarded by their illegal kinship to their owner with an award of freedom, or a grant of his estate. Other slave women and their mixed offspring were not so fortunate but were abandoned after a time and the mother forced to rear such offspring as slaves, or be sold at auction.[39]

35

Intimate relations between white men and slave women not only aroused jealousy and antagonism of white women, but to the wives of the master class, mulatto children were the ever present reminder of the illicit interracial sexual escapades of their brothers, husbands, and sons. Consequently, many a mistress would try to hide, arrange marriage for, or sell such slave mother and/or her children. If they survived their husbands, they would frequently sell or persecute the mulatto child and its mother.[40]

Efforts to Limit or End Slavery

The early 1850s was a period of intersectional strife among the states and territories of Kansas, Nebraska, Missouri, and Louisiana over the limitation or extension of slavery. Pro-slavery southerners fought to expand the institution in opposition to anti-slavery proponents from the north. The state and local courts had long sanctioned slavery in nearly every form since the mid-1600s. However, in 1857 the Supreme Court's historic decision in *Dred Scott* v. *Sanford* further divided the north and south on the issue. There the master of a Missouri slave, Dred Scott, first took Scott to live in the free state of Illinois and thereafter to Northern Louisiana, where the Missouri Compromise barred slavery. Upon returning to Missouri, Scott brought suit to have himself declared a free person on the premise that having taken residence on free land in Illinois, he was thereby liberated from slavery.

Chief Justice Roger B. Taney speaking for the Court held that since the Missouri Compromise was unconstitutional, masters could not lose title to their slaves (property) by taking them anywhere in the Territories. The decision by the highest court in the land was a victory for the south, dampening the hopes and aspirations of slaves and antislavery proponents.[41]

Between 1850 and 1860, intersectional strife among the states and colonies seeking statehood emerged as a result of efforts of southern slaveholders to recover slave fugitives who had escaped to the north. The controversy revolved around who should decide whether slavery should exist or be abolished—the slave states, non-slave states, or the people in each state. When the debate for abolition of slavery tended to gain momentum, slave states threatened to secede from the Union and pro-abolitionists relented to avoid such a result. However, the volatile controversy continued to brew and complicate the question and extent of federal authority.[42]

When the Republicans won the election in November 1860, President Abraham Lincoln assumed office in the midst of the controversy and seven states seceded from the Union, with the potential of eight others following suit.

On April 12, 1861, southern artillery shelled Fort Sumter in the harbor of Charleston, South Carolina. When Lincoln responded with military force, four other states seceded, leaving only Maryland, Delaware, Kentucky, and Missouri members of the Union, and the country submerged in Civil War. Blacks persistently offered themselves for military service but the union repeatedly rejected them. Eventually, in 1862, blacks were accepted and fought in both the Union and Confederate armies. They fought many battles and many lost their lives.[43]

Many slaves were captured during the war and many became free, which resulted in problems of employment and education. Lincoln, therefore, proposed gradual emancipation of the slaves but that was immediately rejected. He then advocated compensated emancipation—paying masters as much as $300 per slave but that was rejected. Lincoln then proposed colonization of free Negroes in Haiti, the Panama area, and Liberia, Africa. He also tried freeing the slaves in rebellious states, but this was met with strong opposition.[44]

Abolition of Slavery

Finally, Lincoln prepared the Emancipation Proclamation in July 1862 but did not issue it until January 1, 1863, declaring all persons held as slaves free forever. That avowal, however, did not free all of the slaves but it applied only to territories under Confederate control and excluded areas under Union control (Tennessee, parts of Louisiana, and Virginia) and border states (Maryland, Delaware, Kentucky, and Missouri). Notwithstanding, the Emancipation Proclamation was a motivating cause for the adoption of the Thirteenth Amendment to the U. S. Constitution ending all slavery on December 18, 1865. It provides:

Section I

Neither slavery nor involuntary servitude, except as a punishment for crime whereof the party shall have been duly convicted, shall exist within the United States, or any place subject to their jurisdiction.

As Stampp concluded, "the survival of slavery cannot be explained as due to the contentment of slaves or their failure to comprehend the advantage of freedom. They longed for freedom. They longed for liberty and resisted bondage as much as any people could have done in their circumstances . . . . "[45] As we have seen in these pages their bondage was kept intact by an elaborate technique of slave control, including vigilantes, with slaveholders having the support and assistance of the state legislatures, the courts, the police, and the militia.

Perhaps the most strikingly incredible feature about the institution of slavery was not solely its dehumanizing brutality and the enduring misery of slaves, but its legal duration of 246 years and three months—from late August 1619 to December 18, 1865. Thus the total duration of blacks in bondage represents either eleven or sixteen generations of enslavement, depending on whether one defines a generation as twenty-one years for legal adult purposes, or fifteen years for child-bearing purposes.

Notes

1. Kenneth M. Stampp, *The Peculiar Institution, Slavery in the Antebellum South* (New York: Alfred A. Knopf, Inc., 1956), 199–204.

2. A. Leon Higginbotham, Jr., *In the Matter of Color, Race and the American Legal Process: The Colonial Period* (New York: Oxford University Press, 1980), 47–48.

3. Stampp, *The Peculiar Institution*, 23.

4. Ibid., 31, 41–43.

5. John Hope Franklin, *From Slavery to Freedom*, 5th ed. (New York: Alfred A. Knopf, Inc., 1980), 133.

6. Stampp, *The Peculiar Institution*, 38–41.

7. Ibid., 46–58.

8. E. Franklin Frazier, *The Negro Family in the United States* (Chicago: University of Chicago Press, 1973), 24–27.

9. Stampp, *The Peculiar Institution*, 59, 60–63.

10. Ibid., 82–83, citing *American Farmer* 2 (1846) and *Southern Cultivator* 2 (1844).

11. Ibid., 78–79, citing William W. Brown, *Narrative of William W. Brown, a Fugitive Slave*, 14.

12. Ibid., 84.

13. Ibid., 85.

14. Ibid., 144.

15. Ibid., 207–08, citing Hekn Tunnicliff Catterall, *Judicial Cases concerning American Slavery and the Negro* (Washington, D.C.: Carnegie Institution of Washington Publication, Papers of the Department of Historical Research, 1937).

16. Ibid., 144–48.

17. Ibid., 149–57.

18. Ibid., 188–89.

19. Ibid., 204–14.

20. Ibid., 190–91.

21. Ibid., 182–92.

22. Ibid., 91, citing *Henry Papers,* William S. Pettegrew to James C. Johnson, January 1847.

23. Ibid., 99, n. 1, citing Frederick Douglass, *My Bondage and My Freedom* (Chicago: Johnson Publishing Company, 1970), 94, 11 and *Farmers Register* (1837), 32, respectively.

24. Ibid., 100–9.

25. Ibid., 103–109.

26. Ibid., 124–29 citing Ulrich B. Phillips, ed., *Plantation and Frontier Documents*, vol. 2 of *Documentary History of American Industrial Society* (Cleveland, Ohio, 1909), 24.

27. Ibid., 110–27.

28. Stampp, *The Peculiar Institution*, 153–54.

29. Ibid., 118.

30. Ibid., 154.

31. Higginbotham, *In the Matter of Color*, 111. Fernow Records, 11–12.

32. Carter G. Woodson, *The Negro in Our History* (Washington, D.C.: Associated Publishers, Inc., 1972), 264. Stampp, *The Peculiar Institution*, 122.

33. Stampp, *The Peculiar Institution*, 130–32.

34. Brewton Berry, *Race Relations* (Boston: Houghton Mifflin Company, 1951), 176.

35. Stampp, *The Peculiar Institution*, 130–32.

36. E. Franklin Frazier, *The Negro Family in the United States* (Chicago: University of Chicago Press, 1973), 36–42.

37. Ibid., 37–42.

38. Ibid., 56.

39. Ibid., 59–61.

40. Ibid., 56.

41. John Hope Franklin, *From Slavery to Freedom: A History of Negro Americans* (New York: Alfred A. Knopf, Inc., 1980), 201–202.

42. Ibid., 199–200.

43. Ibid., 205–207.

44. Ibid., 212–13.

45. Stampp, *The Peculiar Institution*, 139–40.

Three Blacks and Reconstruction

President Lincoln realized early in the 1860s that when the war concluded four million freed blacks would have human needs that required attention. During the war Lincoln was hoping Negroes would elect to emigrate from the United States and he tried unsuccessfully to win congressional cooperation to encourage such a result. He pursued other alternatives only when it became obvious that emigration was not practicable and instead established a number of departments of Negro affairs.[1]

Efforts to Find Family Members

The cessation of the Civil War on April 9, 1865, left the south with great devastation to private dwellings, buildings, factories, and farms. The human population was plagued with widespread disease, starvation, and pervasive political and economic corruption. Four million ex-slaves were freed without any experience in public life.[2] Many newly freed slaves were preoccupied in search of husbands, wives, and children from whom they were separated by sale or other means during slavery.[3] However, the entire period from 1865 to 1900 was a period during which the government tried to provide bare necessities of life for four million ex-slaves and undertake restoration of the south's political and economic life—the period known as "Reconstruction." The period was further characterized by revitalization of the railroads and steel factories, and industrialization of an essentially agrarian economy.[4]

As Union armies assumed control of Confederate territories, they opened schools and undertook the task of educating Negro slaves. They taught them until the schools were later staffed with missionary teachers, teachers from relief societies, and teachers

41

from the later established Bureau of Refugees, Freedmen and Abandoned Lands, which became known as the Freedmen's Bureau. However, the first day school for blacks was established by the American Missionary Association at Hampton, Virginia, in 1861 and Mrs. Mary S. Peak, an educated free woman of color, was its first teacher.[5]

Efforts to educate the freed blacks were nevertheless continued amidst the state of governmental confusion and human hardship. Substantial support for such education came from northern philanthropists. They sent the most able missionary teachers engaged by the Freedmen's Bureau, which was established in the Department of War on March 3, 1865. The Freedmen's Bureau was headed by a commissioner and his assistants in each of the southern states under the administration of the president. Its function was to render assistance to refugees and freedmen in the districts in rebellion or under control of the Union army by supplying them with food, clothing, and medical services, establishing schools, supervising contracts between freedmen and their employers, confiscating and assuming control over southern lands and selling them to freedmen in parcels of not more than forty acres each with a mule, building schoolhouses and asylums for Negroes, and assuming jurisdiction over civil, criminal, and civil rights cases where justice was denied on account of race, color, or previous condition of servitude.

As Woodson and Franklin noted: "The missionary teachers gave their lives as a sacrifice for the enlightenment of the Negro." Although most of the teachers were northern whites, there were a few southern white teachers so engaged. However, the Baptists and Methodists assumed the lead in establishing schools and colleges, such as what is now Shaw University, Raleigh, North Carolina, in 1865, and Morehouse College, Atlanta, Georgia, in 1867. Congregationalists collaborated with the Freedmen's Bureau in having Howard University chartered by the United States government in 1867. Howard was established for the education of all persons regardless of race, and General Samuel C. Howard, commissioner of the Freedmen's Bureau, became its first administrator. The Methodists established Walden, Nashville, Tennessee, in 1865, and several other schools and colleges, including Claflin at Orangeburg, South Carolina, in 1869, and Clark College in

Atlanta in 1870. The American Missionary Association continued establishing schools and colleges including Fisk, Nashville, Tennessee in 1866, Talladega, and others in 1871.[6]

Needless to say, southerners were antagonized by the authority of the bureau and they vehemently opposed its continuation. Notwithstanding, between 1865 and 1869, the bureau relieved considerable suffering of blacks and whites. It had established forty-six or more hospitals and treated more than 450,000 patients. It resettled many persons who had been displaced during the war and the death rate was reduced and sanitary conditions significantly improved.[7]

As early as 1856 the African Methodist Episcopal Church was an independent black church and its membership grew extensively after the war. However, cessation of the war afforded blacks enough freedom to withdraw from the white churches (where they sat in the rear or in a separate building) and establish their own churches. They established the Colored Primitive Baptist, the Colored Cumberland Presbyterian, and the Colored Methodist Episcopal churches. In 1870, the first three black bishops were consecrated by white bishops. All of the black churches played a significant role in providing spiritual and material relief to freed blacks during Reconstruction.[8] Most of them also established and maintained schools and colleges for the education of blacks. By 1867, schools were functioning in nearly every county in each of the confederate states.[9] The black church became and perhaps remained the basic influential social institution in the black community at least through the Civil Rights Movement of the 1960s, if not throughout the entire history of the black population in America.

The Struggle for Governmental Control

When Lincoln was assassinated on April 4, 1865, he was succeeded by Andrew Johnson. Johnson immediately called for a complete abolition of slavery and disenfranchisement in his proclamation of May 1865. He appointed provisional governors of southern states. However, as more Negroes attended school and illiteracy started declining, southern whites became greatly concerned about controlling the freed Negroes. Rumors circulated through communities about uprisings in which Negroes would seek revenge and dispossess whites of their property. In an effort to prevent such eventualities, southern legislatures enacted the so-called Black Codes. The codes, quite similar to the early Slave Codes, were designed to limit areas where Negroes could live, force Negroes to work whether or not they chose to do so, impose penalties for vagrancy, imprisonment for breach of contract if a Negro quit his or her job, prohibit them from testifying in court unless all of the parties to the action were Negro, and imposed fines for delivering seditious speeches, making insulting gestures, violating curfew, being absent from work or in possession of firearms. Certainly Negroes were not enfranchised.[10]

Congress, antagonized by President Andrew Johnson's veto of several bills sponsored by practical Republicans seeking to enlarge their political strength, and northern industrialists seeking cheaper labor in the south passed the Civil Rights Act of 1865 over Johnson's veto. That act was designed to ensure blacks full enjoyment of social and civil privileges. More determined to change the south in retaliation against all resistance, Congress passed the Reconstruction Act on April 9, 1867, wherein the south was divided into five military districts under martial law. Each district was assigned a brigadier general with military support to enforce the laws of the Union and preserve public peace. Negroes were enfranchised in the District of Columbia.

In order for a rebellious state in a military district to extricate itself from the military government, it had to accept the right of suffrage of all male citizens twenty-one years of age without regard to color, race, or previous condition of servitude. In fact, such states would have to ratify the Fourteenth Amendment to the Federal Constitution in 1868. That amendment provided that "No state shall abridge the privileges or immunities of citizens of the United States," "nor deprive any person of life, liberty or property, without due process of law," "nor deny any person the equal protection of the laws." Some of the states readily accepted this option to be relieved of military regime. But Virginia, Georgia, and Texas elected to live with a military government which they deemed more acceptable than the alternative, until they could regain control of the government.[11]

44

The states which accepted the opportunity to relieve themselves of military rule made possible the election of an appreciable number of Negroes to political offices in state governments in the south. Twenty-three Negro representatives served in Congress between 1868 and 1895. Although blacks constituted a majority of the South Carolina government, blacks were never in control of any of the southern state governments. They were, nevertheless, influential in bringing about many positive actions of government.[12]

Economic Plight of Ex-Slaves

In spite of efforts of the Freedmen's Bureau to distribute land among freed blacks, it could not distribute enough land to satisfy the needs of the black population. Consequently, freed blacks gradually returned to the farms under conditions barely better than those which existed during slavery. They were often the disadvantaged partner to a contractual arrangement with their former master for monthly wages or a share of the crops. "Plantation wages ranged from nine to fifteen dollars a month for men and from five to ten dollars for women, in addition to food, shelter, and fuel." Under the sharecropping system, blacks were given a quarter to one-half the cotton and corn, a house (shanty), fuel, and sometimes food. However, at the end of the year the sharecroppers were generally indebted to their employer for most and sometimes for more than they had earned.[13]

The wages paid freed black workers in 1867 were less than wages paid to hired slaves during slavery. The farm labor of freed blacks was a significant contribution to the economic recovery of the South, although their personal gains were minimal. The demographic shift of freed blacks and their acquisition of lands in Alabama, Arkansas, Louisiana, Mississippi, and Florida were made possible by the Southern Homestead Act of 1866. That Act allowed settlers on public lands regardless of race. Some blacks migrated to urban cities in the south and north. However, the migratory dispersion of many freed blacksmiths, cabinetmakers, teachers, bricklayers, pilots, and other skilled craftsmen were met with stern opposition of white artisans when the blacks competed

45

with them for employment. The opposition in many instances resulted in violence in the north and south. Blacks were not favored for membership in labor organizations, and they were virtually excluded from membership until the end of 1880. Because blacks worked for lower wages, they were viewed as strikebreakers, and they lived with that reputation for several generations subsequent to the Civil War.[14]

Freed blacks also tried their hand in various businesses but were generally unsuccessful because they lacked capital and business knowledge. Other blacks, who were successful in business, were eventually victimized by the depression subsequent to the panic of 1873. It should be realized, however, that much of the economic or business failure of blacks was due to the industrial and political transformation through which the American society was passing. Northern industrialists assisted in the reconstruction of the South to enable themselves to exploit Southern resources and take advantage of cheap labor.[15]

Blacks and the Political Process

Perhaps the most monumental results of the reconstruction governments of the south, which comprised many black representatives in Congress, were the establishment of universal free public education and liberalization of the qualifications for voting and holding public office. The Union League of America was established in the north during the Civil War to support the war. After the war the League, which advocated freedom and equal rights, worked with the Freedmen's Bureau and other northern organizations in winning an overwhelming number of blacks for the support of the Republicans. The elimination of southern white men from public life and the effective political control of the south by Washington were viewed by southerners, determined to control their own destiny and freed blacks, as "Radical Reconstruction."[16]

Even prior to "radical [liberal] reconstruction," southerners took their struggle underground by organizing secret and ritualistic organizations such as the Ku Klux Klan, the Jayhawkers, and the Black Horse Cavalry. These organizations augmented the Black Codes by committing outrageous and diabolical night violence against property and persons of the opposition. They engaged in a kind of guerilla warfare against blacks and whites who supported the Washington government. As Franklin noted, their object was "keeping the Negro in his place" and "sniping at Northerners who had come South."[17]

Between 1867 and 1877, other such terrorist organizations as the Knights of the White Camelia, the Pale Faces, the White Brotherhood, the 76 Association, and the Knights of the Ku Klux Klan all fought to acquire absolute control over freed blacks, to drive them and their white allies from power, to end radical reconstruction, and establish what became known as "white supremacy." Armed with weapons (guns and swords), their members disguised themselves and their actions and patrolled parts of the south eluding the Union troops. They utilized force, intimidation, bribery at the polls, ostracism of businesses, arson, and even murder to achieve their mission. The community condoned and supported their activities.[18]

The highest priority of the terrorist groups was to deprive freed blacks of political equality. In order to achieve this priority, freed blacks were run out of town if they failed to comply with orders to refrain from voting. "Insubordinate blacks were whipped, maimed or hanged." Black public officials were given several days to resign office or assume the retributive consequences. Limited efforts on the part of local, state, and congressional authority to suppress the activities of such terrorists groups were unsuccessful, until April 1871, when Congress enacted a law authorizing the president to suspend the writ of habeas corpus (to have the accused brought before court to test the reasonableness of the charge before imprisoning the accused). This was done in order to suppress "armed combinations." The duration of the struggle for political control between southern Democrats and liberal Republicans, freed blacks and the Freedmen's Bureau continued from 1865 until 1877.[19]

Brief Political Freedom Restrained

The ill fate of radical (liberal) reconstruction commenced in 1869 when ex-confederates in Tennessee were enfranchised and a few months later, numerous other Confederates in other south-ern states reclaimed their citizenship by acts of amnesty. Thus the congressional oath disqualifying many ex-Confederates in 1865 was repealed in 1871, and the following year, amnesty restored the franchise to all except about six hundred ex-Confederates. Such amnesty was the beginning of the revival of the democratic party as a growing political influence in the South.

By 1876 the Democrats had resumed political control over most of the south. In some states, like Mississippi, there was considerable bloodshed between the incumbent white-black militia and the new all-white militia of the southern Democrats. Consequently, the radicals were overthrown during 1874 and 1878, not only by southern Democrats resuming political control and implementing conservative government, but also by their own corruption and the intimidation of blacks by white southerners. After the Ku Klux Klan was disintegrated in 1869, the houses and barns of blacks were burned and their crops destroyed. They were whipped and lynched for voting Republican. When blacks began to remain at home on election day, the Democrats won more political control.[20]

Democrats further assured inequality of blacks by excluding them from the primary election procedures that were maintained like private clubs but were in fact the government, and by legal separation of the races. The stagings for the legal racial segregation of blacks were therefore put in place and Tennessee enacted the first modern laws against interracial marriages in 1870, which other states gradually followed. In 1875, Tennessee also enacted the first so-called "Jim Crow" law separating blacks and whites on trains, or wharves, and in depots. Other states enacted similar laws and in 1883 the Supreme Court declared invalid the Civil Rights Act of 1875. Thereafter, blacks were banned from white restaurants, hotels, theaters, and barber shops.

Both the north and south opposed the use of blacks (slave or free) in the military services during the War of Independence. However, both relented in their adamance after November 7, 1775, when Lord Dunmore, governor of Virginia, declared all indentured servants, Negroes, or others, who were able and will-ing to bear arms, could join the British troops and help restore order in the colony. Although earlier in the summer of 1775,

48

General Washington had settled the question about the use of Negro troops by declaring they were not needed, Washington reversed his ruling only after he realized the number by which British troops would increase if numerous slaves ran away and joined the British in the Continental army. Washington then partially reversed his position by permitting the enlistment of free Negroes.

The north relented, and the great loss of slaves to the British troops forced the south to wholly reverse its opposition and enlist Negroes (enslaved or free). Eventually, the north and south were enlisting Negroes for the military services in general.

The slaves fought very well in the war and many distinguished themselves to the extent that few whites could envision them returning to slave status. However, the slave system was so much in demand after the war that the controversy over its existence was made a part of the agenda for debate at the Constitutional Convention in 1787. The crucial debate was about the number of state representatives in Congress. The question raised was whether blacks should be counted in the state population for purposes of determining the numbers of representatives in Congress.

Although most of the north had taken a stand against slavery and advocated the freedom of blacks, many of them still saw slaves as property, and certainly not on human status with themselves. Consequently, they did not think blacks should be counted as a part of the state population to determine the number of representatives each state should have in the House of Representatives.

This dispute resulted in a compromise written into Article I, Section 2 of the Federal Constitution, which in essence provided that representatives and direct taxes shall be apportioned according to the respective numbers, by adding to the whole number of free persons, including indentured servants, but not Indians, and only three-fifths of all other persons (Negroes). Under this formula, two-fifths of all blacks in a state would not be counted as persons in determining the number of state representatives in Congress. This compromise represented the first major legal act of a new federal government to ignore the human existence of numerous blacks in order to limit the number of representatives in Congress from black densely populated districts.[21]

The Democrats made a political issue of the corruption of the radical Republican governments to the discredit and loss of support for the Republicans. The political coalition that existed between poor whites and blacks began to fade. Criminal actions were instituted in 1875 pursuant to the 1870 Enforcement Act to protect the right of blacks to vote in elections. However, the Supreme Court in *United States* v. *Reese* declared the Act unconstitutional, assertedly, because it contained more offenses than were punishable under the Fifteenth Amendment. Also, in *United States* v. *Criskshank,* the Supreme Court construed the Fifteenth Amendment as not guaranteeing citizens the right to vote, but only a right not to be discriminated against on account of race, color, or previous condition of servitude. With such legal decisions in favor of the Southern Democrats, the course was clear for them to conspire to strip blacks of all effective political power by disenfranchising them. The use of armed troops during elections was eliminated by the Congress in 1894. Both political parties competed for black votes and political elections became a period of violence and destruction.[22]

As the Democrats resumed political control in the south, however, they immediately began to contrive various and sundry techniques to circumvent the Fifteenth Amendment and disenfranchise blacks. In 1890, a state constitutional convention was convened in Mississippi where the majority of the population was black. A suffrage provision was adopted imposing a two-dollar poll tax and excluding citizens convicted of burglary, theft, bribery, arson, murder, perjury, or bigamy; and "persons who could not read, understand, or give a reasonable interpretation of any section of the state constitution." The only Negro delegate at the convention, Isaiah Montgomery, said the education and poll tax requirements of the Constitution would disenfranchise 123,000 blacks and only 11,000 whites.

Following Mississippi, South Carolina, led by former senator Ben Tillman, adopted a provision in its constitution for voter qualifications in 1895. The provision required two years' residence, one-dollar poll tax, the ability to read and write, or understand when read aloud, any section of the state constitution, or ownership of property worth three hundred dollars. Convicts were disqualified. Ben Tillman chaired the committee on suffrage during the state's constitutional convention in 1894. John Hope Franklin notes that in advocating disenfranchisement of blacks, Tillman asserted that blacks had done nothing to demonstrate their capacity in government; and black delegate Thomas E. Miller responded that blacks were largely responsible for "the laws relative to finance, the building of penal and charitable institutions, and the greatest of all, the establishment of the public school system . . . ," and numerous reform laws "touching every department of state, county, municipal and town government . . . stand as living witnesses [on the statute books of South Carolina] of the Negro's fitness to vote and legislate upon the rights of mankind . . . ." "Only two whites joined the six Negroes in voting against the constitution of 1895."[23]

Similarly, in 1898 Louisiana introduced in its constitution a new device called the "grandfather clause," which provided that registered voters included "all male persons whose father's and grandfather's were qualified to vote on January 1, 1867." Certainly there were few, if any, Negroes qualified to vote in Louisiana at that time. Other states followed the examples of Mississippi, South Carolina, and Louisiana in disenfranchising blacks. Thus between 1898 and 1910, blacks were essentially disenfranchised throughout the south. Needless to say the south was proud of her achievement of disenfranchising blacks whom they viewed as poor aliens whose ignorance and racial inferiority were not compatible with intelligent and orderly processes of government. However, since most whites realized many blacks would eventually meet the voter qualifications in spite of the constitutional provisions, continued control of the political processes by whites would require additional measures of racial inequality, augmented by hatred and white supremacy.[24]

By 1885, most southern states required separation of the races in schools. Finally, in 1896, the Supreme Court in *Plessey* v. *Ferguson* declared the "separate but equal" doctrine of segregation constitutional. "Separate but equal" meant it was not unreasonable for a state to separate the races for purposes of separation, so long as the facilities of the separation for each race were equal. This decision, by the highest court in the land, represented the omnipotent legal blessing of segregation of the races, which became a visible American way of life—reflecting two worlds—one white, one black for seventy more years.

Thus, it is clear that while Reconstruction was primarily a period of economic and political recovery of the south from the Civil War, black ex-slaves experienced only a brief breath of freedom for about twenty-five years after the war. In other words, although slavery was legally abolished in the deep south on January 1, 1863, and in Union-border states on December 18, 1865, freed blacks enjoyed only freedom of locomotion and some political privileges circumscribed by their severe economic limitations until 1875. At that time, southern legislatures began stripping them of even that limited freedom, by enacting laws requiring the separation of blacks and whites in all public facilities and places of public accommodation. In and after 1885, southern laws required the separation of the races in schools. Thus by 1898 blacks were, for all practical purposes, completely racially segregated from whites in public facilities and accommodations and essentially disenfranchised throughout the south and parts of the north.

Notes

1. John Hope Franklin, *From Slavery to Freedom*, 5th ed. (New York: Alfred A. Knopf, Inc., 1980), 235.
2. Ibid., 227–28.
3. Ibid., 234.
4. Ibid., 299.
5. Carter G. Woodson, *The Negro in Our History* (Washington, D.C.: Associated Publishers, Inc., 1972), 382–83.
6. Ibid., 383–85. Franklin, *From Slavery to Freedom*, 232–33.
7. Franklin, *From Slavery to Freedom*, 235.
8. Ibid., 237.
9. Ibid., 236.
10. Ibid., 223.
11. Woodson, *The Negro in Our History*, 397–402.
12. Franklin, *From Slavery to Freedom*, 244.
13. Ibid., 238–39.
14. Ibid., 239–41.
15. Ibid., 242–43.

16. Ibid., 252–53.
17. Ibid., 235.
18. Ibid., 254.
19. Ibid., 254–55.
20. Ibid., 255–57.
21. Ibid., 86–95.
22. Ibid., 257–58.
23. Ibid., 264.
24. Ibid., 264–65.

Four Segregation in Practice

Although the terms *racial segregation* and *racial discrimination* are sometimes used interchangeably by many Americans, they are not synonymous. Ordinarily, the word *segregation* means: the act of "separating, setting apart or isolating from others."[1]

The word *discrimination* means: (1) the act of making or recognizing a difference or distinction; (2) the act of showing a difference in treatment.[2] In order to have any kind of discrimination there must first exist an observable or recognizable difference or distinction, such as race, religion, nationality or other recognizable characteristic. Secondly, added to that recognizable difference (race), is ascribed an unfavorable significance by one ascribing group or another. Consequently, it is the unfavorable significance which the ascribing group uses as a basis for treating the ascribed group differently. In the United States, black persons with any recognizable degree of African descent, whose heritage derived from slavery in the United States, have been generally ascribed less esteem and human value than whites by slave masters, their children, and many of the white majority who lived long after slavery was abolished.

As previously related in the "slave codes" during slavery and the "black codes" enacted after emancipation, blacks were always socially separated from whites, if not by code, by custom. However, after slavery, apparently something more than code or custom was necessary to keep the races socially separated. In 1865, Mississippi and Florida were the first states to enact laws requiring separation of blacks and whites on public carriers. Tennessee enacted the first "Jim Crow" law in 1875 separating black and white passengers on railroad carriers, depots, and wharves. By 1892, Texas, Alabama, Arkansas, Georgia, Louisiana, and Kentucky had enacted laws requiring separation of whites and blacks on public carriers.[3]

As noted in the previous chapter, the state legislature of Tennessee commenced separating white and black children in schools by law in 1886. With domino effect, other southern states soon followed the practice.

In 1888, Mississippi's Railroad Commission designated separate waiting rooms for whites and blacks. The latter practice was soon extended to all southern terminal restaurants and eating facilities. Between 1907 and 1929, such separation was legally extended by various southern states to include separate cells in prisons, chaining prisoners together, the private and public workplace and their lavatories and drinking water buckets and fountains, to park facilities, and school textbooks. In 1915, Oklahoma authorized its Public Utilities Commission to maintain separate public telephone booths for white and black patrons.[4] Thus, racial segregation "de jure" in the United States meant separating black people from white people pursuant to laws requiring their separation.

"De Jure" segregation received its stamp of approval by the U. S. Supreme Court in the 1896 decision of *Plessy* v. *Ferguson.* Construing the segregation statute of Louisiana requiring separate facilities for Negro and white passengers on railroad trains, the Court established the doctrine of "separate but equal." This meant a state could legally separate the races so long as the facilities for the separated races were of equal quality.

In upholding the constitutionality of the Louisiana statute, Mr. Justice Brown, writing the opinion for the court, said:

> The object of the amendment was undoubtedly to enforce the absolute equality of the two races before the law, but in the nature of things it could not have been intended to abolish distinctions based upon color, or to enforce social, as distinguished from political equality, or a commingling of the two races upon terms unsatisfactory to either . . . .
>
> If the two races are to meet on terms of social equality it must be the result of natural affinities, a mutual appreciation of each other's merit and a voluntary consent of individuals . . . .
>
> If the civil and political rights of both races be equal, one cannot be inferior to the other socially, the Constitution of the United States cannot put them on the same plane.[5]

Subsequently, the 1896 *Plessy* v. *Ferguson* "separate but equal" doctrine, originally applicable to separation of the races on railway trains, was conveniently applied to the races in all schools and all public accommodations throughout the south. However, while the races were always separated, the facilities were always unequal, because the facilities for blacks were invariably inferior to those provided for whites. Consequently, the object or the result of the separation was that blacks were not only separated from the white ruling class of society, but they were also treated unfavorably different. Thus, the separation was itself racially discriminatory. This is what the black lawyers meant in arguing the unconstitutionality of segregated schools before the U.S. Supreme Court in *Brown* v. *Board of Education of Topeka* (1954), when they advocated "separate but equal" is inherently unequal.

"De Facto" (in fact) segregation by race which prevailed largely in the northern United States did not, for the most part, arise from laws requiring separation of the races. Such separation resulted primarily from racial prejudice and discrimination in employment and the cultural deprivation of blacks, as they made the cultural transition from slavery to some measure of freedom, and from southern rural culture to that of the highly industrialized and urban north. Educationally limited, culturally deprived, and economically restricted, most blacks during early migrations north, were isolated in mostly deteriorated pockets of communities in the urban city, as were many members of other ethnic minorities (Jewish, Italian, and Polish immigrants). However, aside from the economic and residential restrictions which were not absolute, blacks and whites generally were not segregated by law for purposes of education, public transportation, or use of publicly supported facilities and public accommodations.

Thus while it appears clear that racial segregation, de jure or de facto, may exist independent of racial discrimination, de jure segregation as we have known it in America has always represented only one form of racial discrimination against blacks. Notwithstanding these distinctions, let us briefly review the operations of those twin-sister institutions—"segregation and discrimination"—as they prevailed in the south and in the north in modified form. Because of the differences in practice, "segregation" will be discussed in this chapter, and "discrimination" in the next chapter.

According to the Bureau of the Census, between 1790, when

56

the first census was taken, and the year 1900, about 90 percent of all blacks resided in the south. Blacks commenced migrating north in significant numbers between 1910 and 1920 when the percentage residing in the south was reduced to 85 percent, and by 1940, to 77 percent. As late as 1963, just prior to passage of the major civil rights legislation, over half (54 percent) of all blacks still resided in the south, while 19 percent migrated to the northeast and 19 percent to the north central United States.

Thus, prior to 1946, over 70 percent of black Americans lived in the southern United States. Of the remaining percentage of blacks who lived in the north and far west, most were at least acquainted with southern racial segregation through visits or contacts with relatives or friends who lived in the south. Consequently, generations of present-day blacks who grew up in the United States prior to the 1960s can well recall the very slow evolutionary social progress of blacks during the era of de jure racial segregation and discrimination throughout the south. It should be interesting to young and older black and white Americans, as well as others unfamiliar with the system of racial segregation by law, to understand how it operated and how it promoted and maintained the concept of white supremacy among numerous white and black Americans for many generations.

Education

Generations of present-day blacks who lived in the south during the years of segregation in education can also vividly recall the legally regimented separation of blacks and whites attending separate state and locally supported public schools and colleges, as well as parochial and other private schools and colleges. They are witnesses to how educational facilities for blacks were generally overcrowded, ill-equipped, and substantially inferior compared to schools for whites. They recall how white students received and used new books that years later were transferred to black schools for black students and how many county black children had to walk miles to school while most county white children rode school buses to and from school. After the teaching staffs in all black schools became all black during the early 1900s, black teachers in many communities were paid less than their white counterparts who taught in only white schools and colleges, although both were paid by the same tax-supported state or local governmental authority.

As late as 1945, less than forty-four years ago, southern states were spending two times as much on the education of each white child than they spent on each black child. They invested four times as much in white school plants as in black school plants, and paid white teachers a salary 30 percent higher than black teachers. Four times as many whites finished high school as blacks.[6]

One year earlier, in 1944, seventeen segregation-practicing states spent $42 million busing white children, and a little more than one million busing black children to and from school. In 1947, such states "spent $86 million of public funds on white colleges and five million on black colleges," leaving blacks without anything near a first-class public university opportunity for higher learning.[7]

No competition in athletics or any other kind of recreational or scholastic activity took place between black and white schools and colleges. In some cities like Charleston, South Carolina, white and black school pupils going to and returning from school were assigned separate sides of the streets on which to walk by a motorcycle police officer. This practice was instituted reportedly to prevent white and black pupils from colliding with one another and thereby becoming engaged in a fist fight. With or without that practice, it was commonplace for white pupils to yell "niggers" to black pupils, and for black pupils, in retaliation, to yell "crackers" to the white pupils. Thus, a familiar ring of the times from white children was "nigger, nigger ring the bell," with the retort from black children, "cracker, cracker go to hell." With such racial animosity and isolation, it was common for either a white or a black child to become an adult without ever having had a single childhood acquaintance or even having known the name of a single child of the opposite race.

Qualified black high school graduates could not attend state and locally supported southern colleges and universities originally established for whites. This was so, even though such institutions were supported by tax dollars to which blacks contributed their share. Nor could blacks attend privately supported institutions of higher learning. Instead, to assure continued separation of the races, each southern state government established at least one state college for blacks. These institutions initially focused on agricultural and mechanical training. They were substantially less equipped than institutions for whites, and for many years, several were not accredited by Regional Accrediting Associations.

For many years prior to 1960 the great majority of black colleges and universities did not offer graduate programs for advance degrees. Meharry Medical School in Nashville, Tennessee, and Howard University in Washington, D.C., were the only two which offered professional degrees in medicine and dentistry. Only Howard offered degrees in law and engineering. Black college graduates could not be admitted to southern state or private colleges or universities to pursue undergraduate, graduate, or professional degrees in medicine, law, dentistry, engineering, or other academic disciplines. However, they could apply to their respective southern states for financial assistance, and such states would pay their tuition to an out-of-state (northern, black or white) college or university to which they had been accepted for admission. Such southern state governments preferred to pay the black applicant's tuition to other institutions of higher learning, rather than make exception to their apartheid system of education for white and black students.

The disparity in facilities and quality in secondary educational opportunity prevailed in the south until the decision in *Brown* v. *The Board of Education of Topeka* (1954) which was pending three years (1951–54) before the Supreme Court. During that three-year period, southern legislatures, sensing the death knell of de jure segregated schools, made a diligent effort to equalize the educational facilities by building and renovating one school after another for blacks. Before, and just subsequent to the Court's decision, there were numerous recently built and renovated schools for blacks in communities throughout the south. In some instances, the newly built schools for blacks were superior to those which existed and those recently built for whites. The sudden availability of funds appropriated for school construction represented the only good-faith effort on the part of white southern governments to equalize educational facilities for blacks. Of course, this was a last-minute effort to spare themselves the agony of integrating whites and blacks in schools.

The Silver Lining

If there ever was any truth in the old familiar cliche, "Every cloud has a silver lining," perhaps the silver lining in de jure segregated schools for blacks was the several educational "hallmarks" which the apartheid system itself produced and maintained. Notwithstanding the racial isolation and general substandard quality education in many of the formerly ill-equipped southern black schools, it should be recognized that there were several exceptional public and private black community schools, and a few black colleges and universities in the nation, which provided standard, and in a few cases, superior quality education. Perhaps the most notable of these was Dunbar High School of Washington, D.C. Dunbar was established in 1870 and for most of its years housed in its First Street, N.W., building. It was reportedly the first high school in the United States built exclusively for blacks. Evidence of its excellence in education can be measured by some of the same criteria by which the academic standing of any school is judged.

According to a study of the IQs of nearly 70 percent of Dunbar students in the days of legal segregation, Dunbar students scored in the normal or above-average range, while 18 percent scored 115 and above. Dunbar was the first school in Washington, D.C., if not the first black high school in the nation, to receive a chapter of the National Honor Society. Approximately three out of four of its graduates went to college. Though most of them went to black colleges or universities because of the economic limitations of their families and racial practices of many white colleges and universities, quite a few of them did go to Ivy League institutions such as Harvard and Amherst, where several graduated with honors. Dunbar's alumni proudly boast of its long list of notable graduates such as General Benjamin O. Davis, Sr., the first black general in the U.S. Army, the late Honorable William Hastie, the first black federal judge, Dr. Charles Drew, the discoverer of blood plasma, the Honorable Edward Brooke of Massachusetts, the first black senator since Reconstruction, and many others, including a host of commissioned military officers in the armed forces during and after World War II.[8]

Even though Dunbar was not provided adequate space and other educational facilities equivalent to those in most white schools, its faculty (owing to their exclusion from white schools and numerous other areas of employment) consisted of exceptionally qualified black men and women. Most of them held master's or doctorate degrees from leading white colleges and universities, and who, but for their ethnicity, would have been teaching in white schools and colleges, or employed in executive jobs throughout the nation's business enterprises or federal, state and local governments.[9]

While exceptional black high schools in other southern communities may not have been as richly endowed with teaching and administrative staffs as highly qualified as Dunbar's, virtually all of them had some highly qualified and outstanding teachers, with a complement of adequate teachers and administrators who made a significant difference in educating black students because they cared about all students. Complementing the teachers and administration was a high percentage of reasonably disciplined black students. To a lesser degree, all such high schools and a few black institutions of higher learning had some of the same characteristics which made Dunbar outstanding. All of them can point with pride to a substantial number of successful and outstanding graudates. Some such high schools were:

Booker T. Washington High School
    in Atlanta, Georgia, of which Dr. Martin Luther King, Jr., and a host of other notables were graduates.
Armstrong High School (technical),
    of Washington, D.C.
Garnet High School,
    of Charleston, West Virginia, from which the Rev. Leon H. Sullivan, of O.I.C., and Tony Brown, of "Tony Brown's Journal," were graduated.
Booker T. Washington High School
    of Norfolk, Virginia.

Eliza Miller High School of
  Helena, Arkansas.
Booker T. Washington High School
  of Tulsa, Oklahoma.
Frederick Douglass High School
  of Oklahoma City.

Certainly there were other equally effective public black schools of all levels in other southern and northern communities.

In addition to such exceptional black public high schools, were several reputable black private high schools in the south which also produced their share of high achievers. Some of them were Avery Institute in Charleston, South Carolina; boarding schools such as Palmer Memorial Institute in Sedalia, North Carolina; Barber Scotia in Concord, North Carolina; St. Emma's Institute (military) in Rock Castle, Virginia, and Mather Academy in Camden, South Carolina. Today, blacks familiar with these public and private black schools often talk with pride about some of the advantages they had over northern integrated schools of that era and the growing concern of deteriorating white and black schools of today. There appears to be a consensus among blacks who attended such schools that the teaching staffs of the old segregated public and private schools taught students "black" history, explained how and why the status of blacks was largely what it was at that time in America, inspired self-confidence, and helped develop self-esteem in their students. They eternally emphasized the importance of education and good scholarship as dire necessities to cope with and overcome the obstructions of racism in America.

Older blacks also seem to agree that the old all-black schools, and colleges, too, served as a forum or incubator that provided a greater opportunity for the development of black leadership, culture, and pride. In other words, black students had an unhampered opportunity to be elected to school offices, to become homecoming or class queens, to gain membership in honor societies, and become athletic managers, et cetera, without consideration of race. Many blacks contend it is for these reasons that the great majority of the older black leadership in nearly every American community is a product of the segregated system of education. If these observations are correct, as the evidence appears to indicate, then it is safe to conclude that, in spite of much substandard education in black schools and colleges of the old south, there were some significant redeeming benefits from which blacks, as a whole, profited.

Public Transportation

Subsequent to the decision in *Plessy* v. *Ferguson* (1896), interstate common carriers, honoring segregation of the races, gradually required black passengers on all public local buses or trolley car transportation throughout the south to sit (load) from the rear towards the front of the coach, and white passengers to sit (load) from the front towards the rear of the coach. The bus driver, who was always white, would enforce the law by ordering passengers to move to a seat in accordance with the system. If a black passenger refused to comply with the driver's order, the driver would refuse to move the bus or trolley and would call the police. The police, in just about all cases, would arrest the black passenger for disorderly conduct or disturbing the peace. If the bus or trolley first had a full capacity of white passengers, whites would be allowed to occupy each available seat. If the reverse situation occurred, blacks were accorded the same seating. However, if white passengers entered the bus under the latter circumstances, or all of the front seats were occupied by whites, some bus drivers would order black passengers to get up and stand in the aisle to accommodate the seating of the new white passengers.

In order to avoid any misunderstanding in complying with the system, some cities like New Orleans, Louisiana, provided a movable sign labeled WHITE on one side and COLORED or NEGRO on the other, which was mounted on the top of the back of a passenger seat midway of the bus or trolley coach. The passengers could move the sign backward or forward in accordance with the racial composition of the passengers.

When black and white passengers were traveling long distances by commercial buses (Greyhound-Trailway) in southern states, the same procedure of racial separation was enforced. However, when traveling by train, a compartmental or full train coach was designated for black passengers which was always the first passenger car behind the locomotive, or mail or baggage car. At this location the black passengers were less likely to come in contact with white passengers and they were the first passengers to receive the immediate impact of coal cinders from the old steam locomotive, as well as the best audio reception of the locomotive whistle and engine noise. This coach was often overcrowded with elderly people, babies, and young children either migrating to the north, or going north or south and returning from visiting relatives and friends or transacting business.

Although most black passengers carried a home-prepared box lunch, those who could afford to eat in the dining car could do so. The first two tables, one on each side of the aisle as you entered the car, were separated by a curtain and reserved for black dining passengers only. With this arrangement, the white dining passengers generally had to pass through the black dining section to enter and exit the remaining section reserved for white diners. The black diners could enter and exit the dining car without having to pass or be seen by the white dining passengers.

Only a minority of blacks could afford first-class Pullman coach service. However, a black could purchase a ticket for such service in the north and become a Pullman passenger, but would most likely be reassigned from Pullman to passenger coach service when the train entered a southern state.

When northbound trains arrived at the first terminal in the first northern state that did not require separation of the races, white and black passengers could remain seated or move to any available seat in any passenger coach of their choice. Also at this juncture, black passengers could be seated and served at any table in the dining car. However, it was most interesting to observe a southbound passenger train enter the last northern terminal before entering a southern state which required racial separation. White passengers seated in the first coaches, thereafter designated for blacks, had to take their baggage and move to an available seat in any of the several passenger cars, thereafter reserved for white passengers. Correspondingly, all black passengers not seated in the first coaches had to take their baggage and move to the first passenger coaches, thereafter reserved for black passengers. New black and white passengers boarding the train at this time had to comply with this arrangement. Thus, one could observe the effective and uniform compliance with this procedure by standing on the boarding platform at Union Station in the Nation's capital, Washington, D.C., or on the boarding platform in Union Train Terminal in Cincinnati, Ohio, which were ideal locations from which to observe the classical operation of interstate-passenger-train racial transition.

Prior to the mid-1960s practically all train, bus, and airline terminals in the south had separate waiting rooms for black and white passengers. Some terminals did not have a waiting facility for blacks and blacks had to wait outside. Generally, bus terminals for interstate busline companies, like Greyhound and Trailway, maintained a makeshift and much smaller waiting room for blacks. The black waiting room was generally adjacent to the side or rear of the much larger and main terminal waiting room reserved for whites. There was usually a small ticket window in the black waiting room which adjoined the inner side or rear of the main ticket office of the white waiting room through which black ticket-purchasers were served by a common ticket agent for both white and black passengers.

However, one of the most humiliating experiences black bus patrons had to tolerate was standing at the little ticket window where the white ticket agent could always see them, and watch the agent wait upon one white ticket-purchaser after another who entered the terminal after the blacks were at the window awaiting service. Black prospective passengers, familiar with the service, knew the worst thing they could do was to call the ticket agent. In such an event, the agent would often tell them in discourteous and often profane language, not to rush him or her, and would proceed to take his or her good time in waiting upon them. Many times when a waiting black ticket-purchaser was finally sold a ticket, all of the seats on the bus (for whites and/or blacks) would have been occupied.

Similarly, in all train, bus, and airline terminals, department stores, as well as some five-and-dime stores throughout the south, it was common to see pairs of restrooms and drinking fountains often located side by side, one labeled WHITE, the other COLORED, or NEGRO. "Negro" was often spelled with a small "n."

Public Accommodations

Perhaps the greatest inconveniences imposed by the practice of racial segregation and discrimination in public accommodations were those encountered in non-local travel by blacks traveling long distances in the south by automobile. Prior to passage of the Civil Rights Act on public accommodations in 1964, many blacks migrating north or simply traveling north or south on business, vacation, or any emergency often did so by automobile. For most people this was the cheapest mode of transportation for transporting either several passengers or small furnishings. There were few or virtually no black-owned restaurants, hotels, motels, or tourist homes where blacks could lodge and eat, and all white operated restaurants, hotels and motels refused to serve or accommodate black persons in compliance with the laws requiring separation of the races. In fact, many of such establishments in the north would refuse black patronage even though they generally were not honoring laws to do so. A few of the restaurants or eating establishments provided a rear or side window or counter at which they would sell blacks a brown bag lunch to take along with them.

Blacks considering a long-distance trip by automobile through the south had to think and plan like a soldier preparing to go on bivouac. Many of them learned it was wise to get a good night's sleep and prepare for a continuous and often non-stop journey from point of departure to ultimate destination. If there were no alternate drivers, the only driver would have to safely pull off the highway and take a nap for an hour or two. Occasionally, the journey would pose an additional risk of life and limb if a hurricane or snowstorm were encountered or if the roads suddenly became hazardous due to fog or ice. One can only wonder how many blacks may have met death or serious injury as a result of having to continue their journey under adverse weather conditions, simply because hotels or other public accommodations were not available to them.

Nevertheless, preparation for the journey usually required packing a box-lunch with beverages in a thermos bottle or other container, drinking water, a flashlight, and a roll of toilet tissue. However, nature and foresight dictated that the passengers not eat or drink too much because it was already necessary for them to have enduring bowels and a strong bladder since toilet accommodations were generally not available to them. The majority of gasoline stations did not have dual (white and black) lavatory accommodations and very few of them would permit blacks to use their facilities reserved for whites. Occasionally, some service station proprietors would allow blacks to use lavatories reserved for whites if there were no white patrons present. Hence, it was not uncommon to hear blacks tell about how they had to stop along a deserted road to allow their female passengers to go into the bushes first, and then their male passengers for a comfort stop.

Lodging at Southern Destination

Most blacks traveling south generally knew before their departure where they would be lodging at their destination since public accommodations were not available to them. If they were not a guest of relatives or friends, they often knew they could contact the YMCA, the YWCA, the Urban League, a church, or a civic or other community-based organization. Such organizations generally maintained a list of names and addresses of reputable blacks who owned or rented homes with extra bedrooms, adequate toilets, and sometimes eating facilities, who would accept travelers as guests for a modest fee of three, four, five, or seven dollars a day. Such arrangements were also made for black artists, athletes, or participants in a conference or convention. Sometimes certain members of the community prepared and served meals for a nominal sum. Of course these were days when the very great majority of Americans were law-abiding, reasonably trustworthy, and decent. Thus blacks offering their accommodations on such occasions assumed virtually no risk at all. A general spirit of cooperation and kinship prevailed among most blacks under the circumstances of segregation.

Movie Theaters

For the most part, whites and blacks attended the same movie theaters after purchasing their tickets for admission from generally separate ticket-booth agents and entering the theater through separate entrances. Frequently blacks entered through a side street entrance and ascended stairs to a small balcony reserved for blacks only or sat in the rear of a one-floor-level theater. If a white or black person tried to purchase a ticket for admission at the wrong ticket window, the agent would simply refuse to sell him or her a ticket and advise him or her of the law requiring separation of the races. Except for a very few amateur and substantially all-black-cast movies, virtually all of the movies consisted of a white cast. Occasionally, a black would perform in a supporting role as a subordinate, a comedian, or an entertainer. Perhaps, the only thing equal about the whole arrangement of movies as a source of entertainment was the price for admission.

Celebrity Artists

Whenever celebrity entertaining artists appeared in southern communities, they did so before segregated audiences. If black artists like Marian Anderson, Paul Robeson, Louis Armstrong, Cab Calloway, or Ella Fitzgerald came to town, they performed first on one evening for the white audience and on another evening for the black audience. The same arrangement was followed if there were any white artists for whom there was black mass appeal. They appeared for the white audience first, and then for the black audience. In a few situations involving classical concerts or plays, a few segregated seats were sometimes reserved for blacks in a balcony or at the rear of a theatre or auditorium. Otherwise, there were no provisions for blacks to see such artists at all.

Carnivals and Parks

During the carnival season of the year, usually the largest carnival came to town one week and constructed their equipment on public grounds reserved for whites. The second week following, a smaller, less equipped carnival came to town and constructed their equipment on a black recreational field and opened business for black patrons. Only one circus came to town for whites and blacks, but there was a separate seating section for blacks.

In the larger southern communities there were separate parks, athletic fields, and playgrounds for whites and blacks. In either case, the parks, fields or playgrounds for whites were of better quality and better equipped than those provided for blacks. Only a few white playgrounds or schools had gymnasiums and swimming pools and even fewer black schools or parks had such public facilities. In many smaller communities there were no such recreational facilities for blacks, and black youths had to play in open fields or vacant lots. If they lived near water (creeks, lakes, or rivers) they often learned to swim and swam in such waters. Parks for whites often had signs at their entrances which read: "No dogs and negroes [or niggers] allowed."

Medical Care

Before 1950, although many hospitals in the north and south sometimes had a few black nurses on their staffs, almost none of them (north and south) had a single black physician on their medical staff. Acceptance of black physicians on the medical staffs of northern white hospitals was for all practical purposes non-existent prior to 1950. More frequently than not, black physicians were not permitted to utilize the operating and laboratory facilities of such hospitals. In most cases black physicians were confined to the staffs and use of facilities of black-owned or operated hospitals, if there were any.

Prior to 1945, most hospitals in the United States had general wards for female patients and general wards for male patients. However, where patients were separated by race as they were throughout the south, the hospitals maintained a general ward for white females, a general ward for white males, a general ward for black females, and a general ward for black males. In many small communities the black wards were often in poorly kept basements, or the ground floor of hospitals. In virtually every instance, the wards reserved for blacks, as well as the patient attention, quality of services, and bedside manner, were substantially less acceptable than those provided for whites. This was especially true in publicly supported hospitals whose support was partially supplied by blacks as taxpayers. In many rural areas and small communities where hospitals could not provide adequate separate facilities, black patients were not admitted to the hospital except in mostly life-or-death situations, and even then, they were treated in makeshift rooms separate from white patients.

Prior to 1955 there was a very small ratio of black physicians to black patients in the entire United States. Virtually no community in the country had sufficient black physicians for the treatment of its black patient population. That may still be true today to a lesser degree. Numerous communities and some whole counties throughout the south did not have a single black physician. Consequently, private medical services for a very substantial number of black patients in all southern communities were dependent upon the mercy and grace of white private physicians.

Many white physicians refused to treat black patients under any circumstances. However, white physicians who treated black patients generally did so in accordance with the laws, mores, and folkways of racial separation, by having office hours for white patients on certain days and office hours for black patients after regular hours, or on different days. Other physicians did so by maintaining a waiting room for white patients and a waiting room for black patients. When the latter was the case, both waiting rooms usually had separate entrances. Often each waiting room adjoined a different side of the doctor's examining office, with each waiting room having a door through which patients could enter and exit the examining office. With this arrangement, the doctor could often treat a white or black patient without either patient seeing or even knowing that the other had been seen by the doctor. However, black patients sometimes knew from the duration of their wait, or from having overheard voices in the examining room, that some doctors invariably saw several if not all of the white patients before they would see their black patients. Many black patients living in counties and small or rural communities sometimes had to travel as much as one hundred miles or more to obtain scarce medical services by a physician, simply because many white physicians would not treat, or adequately treat them.

The Military Services

Although blacks served in the army and fought in most of America's major wars, including the Civil and Spanish-American wars, they did so in segregated companies and regiments nearly always under the command of white commissioned officers. In both the Civil and Spanish-American wars, whites in command tried to prevent the use of blacks in combat. The same effort was made in World War I and World War II. Nevertheless, when those in command finally relented to the efforts of blacks to be involved in combat, they were generally forced to do so by the state of the battle which might well have made a difference between victory and defeat. Blacks served in the navy as stewards, mess attendants, and cooks until 1942, when World War II necessitated their admission into the largest and principal naval function, the seaman branch.

Likewise, the Marine Corps, which is a part of the navy, was not open to blacks until the first companies of blacks were trained at Camp Lejeune, North Carolina, during the early years of World War II. The army air force accepted the first black cadets for pilot training in 1940. Between 1942 and 1943, black women entered the women's auxiliary services and served in segregated units. Blacks in all branches of the military service, whether in training or battle, were always separated as a unit as much as possible.

Separation Nearly Absolute

The physical and conscious separation of the races in the south could not possibly have been more universal. When World War II ended in 1945, the governors of all states, the mayors of all cities, and since Reconstruction, all elected and appointed officials of all states and local governments in the south were white. All federal, state, and local judges sitting in the south, all members of the state militia or National Guards, state highway patrol, county sheriff, and the local police force in practically every southern community were white. Prior to 1945, the journalism staffs of essentially all newspapers and the news reporting staffs of all radio and television stations were white. Likewise, the tellers, cashiers, clerks, and officers in all banks and other business establishments, except in the few black-owned and operated banks and other businesses were all white.

All churches and other religious organizations, including the YMCAs and YWCAs, provided separate buildings and services for whites and blacks.

So consciously oriented to the legal mandate of separation of the races were southern whites and blacks that both not only reacted automatically in compliance with its edict, but separation came to mean not only physical separation, but that whites were always first and blacks were always last and overtly accorded less respect. The consistency of this practice and understanding over the years further solidified the concept of white supremacy among most white and many black persons. Thus, this common understanding and practice resulted in a well established unwritten code of interracial etiquette, which was generally followed by whites and tolerated by blacks for many generations. Consequently, the humiliation and degradation of blacks from the combined systems of segregation, discrimination and interracial etiquette were manifested in nearly every aspect of southern everyday living.

Prior to the era of self-service supermarkets and take-a-check-number service in grocery or other stores, the all-white clerks almost without exception automatically acknowledged the presence of whites and invariably served them first, even though blacks were first awaiting their services. On many occasions blacks had to wait until several whites who came after them had been waited upon before the clerk would acknowledge their presence and serve them. Even if a white clerk on some occasions attempted to wait upon a black person in turn, some white persons would insist that the clerk serve them first. In such cases, the clerks would generally yield to the demands of the white patrons for fear of losing their job, or of losing their white patron's business. Occasionally, a white person would tell the white clerk to serve the black patron who had preceded him or her.

When it was time to pay the bill after making a purchase of merchandise of one kind or another, white clerks often held out their hand and accepted the money from the black patron. In returning change, however, the clerks often laid the change on the counter. Courageous blacks would spare themselves this discourtesy by placing their money on the counter, not holding out their hand, but await the clerk's return of their change to the counter.

Perhaps one of the few services for which blacks and whites formed the same line and were waited upon in turn was for services of a teller in a bank and a clerk in the post office. Other and almost daily indignities and humiliation experienced by blacks included the common practice of most whites of any age, refusing to address a black man as "Mister" and a black woman as "Miss" or "Mrs.," as by southern custom white men and women were so addressed. Instead, black men 21 to 125 years of age were addressed by most whites of any age by their first name, a nickname, or, if first name or nickname were unknown, frequently referred to as "Boy." Likewise, black women of any age were addressed by most whites of any age, by their first name, a nickname (Mammy), and not infrequently referred to as "Girl" or "Gal." Of course, on the slightest provocation, and sometimes without any provocation, all blacks were privately or publicly called "niggers."

It was a common practice for many white persons to consciously release the swinging doors of a department or five-and-dime store in the face of a black person only one or two feet behind them. Such conduct was in accord with the southern orientation of whites to hate, disrespect, and humiliate blacks. To do otherwise, was by southern custom, extending a courtesy to blacks to which they were not entitled.

Many blacks still comment about the frequent coincidences of how many white bus drivers (north and south) used to approach a bus stop where black and white prospective passengers were waiting two, three or four abreast, and accurately stop the entrance door of the bus directly in front of whites, enabling them to enter the bus first; how some clothing stores would not permit black patrons to try on items of clothing before they purchased them; and how it was taboo for black and white persons (especially a black man and a white woman) to walk on the streets or sit side-by-side on the same seat in an automobile. It was not unusual to see a white man or woman transporting their black domestic servant to or from their home, with the family dog sitting on the passenger side on the front seat, and the black servant sitting on the rear seat of their automobile.

It was not unusual for white persons to block the sidewalks while engaged in conversation or to walk two, three, or four abreast and fail to move or yield for an approaching black person to pass them without walking around them, even if it meant the black person had to step off the sidewalk to do so. Most blacks believed this was done intentionally in an effort to make or keep blacks status conscious of who was in charge. More often than not, blacks would walk around white males under such circumstances to avoid a verbal of physical confrontation because they knew they were subject to be the victim of verbal or violent physical abuse, and also face the probability of arrest and conviction in accordance with southern justice. The same set of circumstances posed an even greater risk of physical harm if the white males obstructing the walkway were under the influence of alcohol, as was sometimes the case. Under the latter circumstances most blacks were taught to cross to the other side of the street, to take a detour, or run.

Blacks familiar with the south knew that generally a group of white men under the influence of alcohol in any setting almost always posed a humiliating or unsafe situation for blacks. Most blacks, especially young females, were taught to get away from such a situation even if it meant running, because it was generally under such circumstances that members of the white male group would instigate a confrontation by calling blacks "niggers" or other abusive appellations, if not attacking them outright physically, sometimes including raping black women and girls.

Southern interracial etiquette was simply a modified survival of the "technique of slave control" previously discussed in chapter II. Most whites and blacks had come to understand it as a standard of behavioral propriety whenever a member of either race was in the presence of the other. Whites understood they were not to respect or treat blacks as equals and blacks understood they would not be treated as equals—sometimes not even as humans and that blacks in turn were to be submissive to such treatment. Blacks also understood that their failure to appear to overtly accede to and actually comply with such standards would result in their being socially branded a "smarty," or "uppity nigger," probably subjecting them to such reprisals as denial of credit, loss of employment, or being blacklisted for employment, framed for criminal conduct, and sometimes the victim of outright violence against their person.

On the contrary, whites understood their options and their authoritative duty to impose such sanctions for failure of blacks to cooperate with the established racial standards of conduct. While all southern whites did not exercise their options, enough of them did to enable the practices to prevail for many generations. In fact, any white person who openly criticized the established standards of interracial conduct, or refused to cooperate and comply with the system, was branded "a nigger lover." In describing the consistency and occasional relaxation of these practices by whites, and the penalty for their failure to comply, Berry said:

> The etiquette of race relations in the south is a highly complex ritual, and is not mastered overnight. There are even occasions when the rules are set aside, if one knows how, when and where. Violations of the ritual on the part of whites are an invitation to reproach, ranging from ridicule and gossip to ostracism and even bodily harm.[10]

Inhibited Social Assimilation

Although blacks had always been socially separated from whites during slavery, it is clear that legal segregation of the races in other activities of life after slavery was designed to prevent social equality, interracial sexuality or marriage, and to maintain white supremacy and control over American blacks. Having largely achieved that objective, legal segregation was also the instrument by which the rate and degree of cultural assimilation of the majority of blacks was significantly impeded.

Noted sociologists have long observed that annihilation or expulsion is not necessarily the usual outcome of contact between races. They acknowledge that "more common by far is the fusion of the two (assimilation . . .)."[11]

Whites in the United States learned early with the American

Indians that whenever there is contact between different races, conflict inevitably ensues. In an effort to avert such conflict, an unsuccessful effort was made by American whites to force cultural assimilation of the American Indian ". . . to integrate him into American society."[12]

It would appear that the efforts of the American missionaries and the Freedmen's Bureau were certainly efforts not only to educate, but also to bring about the cultural assimilation of blacks into the American society. The efforts of the bureau were of very short duration (seven years—1865–1872) and those of the missionaries very limited compared to the growing size of the black population. However, aside from the brief and inadequate efforts of both, blacks are the only known Americans whose rate and degree of cultural assimilation were effectively restrained by laws requiring or upholding segregation and discrimination until the enactment of the modern civil rights laws during 1964–68.

Notes

1. *Webster's New World Dictionary*, 2d. ed., s.v. "segregation."
2. Ibid., s.v. "discrimination."
3. Derrick A. Bell, Jr., *Race, Racism and American Law* (Boston: Little Brown and Company, 1973), 205.
4. Ibid., 206–207.
5. *Plessey* v. *Ferguson*, 163 U.S. 256, 258, 261 (May 18, 1896).
6. Richard Kluger, *Simple Justice* (New York: Random House, 1975), 256–57.
7. Ibid., 257.
8. Thomas Sowell, "Dunbar: Historic Love," *Tony Brown's Journal* (September 1983).
9. Ibid.
10. Brewton Berry, *Race Relations* (Boston: Houghton Mifflin Company, 1951), 281.
11. Ibid., 215.
12. Ibid., 20.

Five   Discrimination in Practice

Prior to 1942, America's great democracy was blighted by the obvious discriminatory and deprived status to which its black citizens had been relegated by government and social custom. This obvious contradiction in democracy and religion always struck the immediate attention of foreign citizens and dignitaries visiting the United States. While there was always conflict between the black minority and white majority races, the onset of World War II, the attendant draft of young men into the armed forces, the demand for labor in industries essential to the war effort, as well as apprehension about the duration and unknown outcome of the war by the American people aggravated the conflict between the races and highlighted the dilemma in which they found themselves.

It was during this initial global conflict that Dr. Frederick P. Heppel, former president of Carnegie Corporation, solicited the services of the distinguished Swedish socio-economist Gunnar Myrdal. Mr. Myrdal was commissioned to conduct a study on what was called "The Negro Problem in America," and have his findings published at the expense of the Carnegie Corporation. Myrdal was selected for this task because of his scholarly ability, but also because his racial objectivity might have been spared obscurity by his foreign heritage. The study was completed and published in 1942 in two volumes titled *An American Dilemma.*[1]

In previous chapters we have seen the extent to which blacks were separated by law, custom and economic circumstances, from essentially all meaningful social interaction with the American white population—in the south and up north. The reader can venture an estimation of the degree to which the acculturation of a majority of the black population was inhibited, by separating, particularly black persons from the white population in the United

States. In this chapter we will review several other kinds of racial discrimination which further restricted the cultural growth and economic progress of many black Americans.

Economic Discrimination

Considering all of the inhibiting forms of racial discrimination imposed upon blacks, perhaps none did more to restrict their social progress than deprivation of quality education and economic opportunity—employment and business.

As Myrdal observed, since blacks were owned as property during slavery, that caste system of human property remained after the slaves were emancipated. Consequently, blacks in every generation were disadvantaged at the start, and discrimination against them was "rooted in this tradition of economic exploitation." Moreover, this attitude, continued by whites, was justified by false racial beliefs premised upon a semblance of evidence of low standards of efficiency, ambition, reliability, and morals of the black population. Myrdal said, "That is what the white man sees, and he opportunistically exaggerates what he sees." Conceding that such deficiencies are not inborn in blacks, at least in no significant degree, he concluded that such deficiencies are caused directly or indirectly by the very poverty he was attempting to explain, as well as discrimination in education, public health, legal protection and other aspects of life.[2]

Analyzing the complex scheme of causative interrelated factors of black poverty with a view towards developing a practicable plan to raise the income level of blacks, Myrdal observed that the dynamics of the problem are such that:

A principal change which affects any one of the collection of interdependent causitive factors (1) economic level; (2) standards of intelligence, education, health, manners, decency, ambition and morals; and (3) discrimination by whites, will trigger changes in the prior two through mutual interaction, and cause the whole system to automatically move one direction or the other. No one factor is the cause, in a theoretical sense.[3]

Concluding upon the above analysis, Myrdal said the system of slavery was replaced essentially by a system of sharecropping; that the latter system was as poverty ridden as the former; and that it is exceedingly difficult for one to work himself out of poverty under another system of poverty. In other words, "Poverty itself breeds the conditions which perpetuate poverty."[4] The above analysis can be observed today in undeveloped nations in Africa, India, and South America.

Explaining the history of why blacks were still poor in 1943, Myrdal said:

> Blacks have been in a dependent position and exploited, as a farmer. They were tied to cotton agriculture, which at one time yielded instant wealth to whites, but now forces blacks and other surplus workers to leave lands of the south. In the city, blacks were kept out of jobs, especially the good ones, and have seldom had the opportunity to prepare themselves adequately for jobs which required superior skill or professional training. They are isolated in slums by residential segregation more consistently than their purchasing power necessitates. Finally, blacks do not share equally in free services with their fellow citizens afforded by the government.[5]

In 1943, the typical black farm family had an income considerably lower than the average white farm family. The family incomes of normal black families in southern villages were less than three hundred dollars in 1935–36, while the median income for normal white families was twelve hundred dollars. The differential was similar in small and large cities even though the income of black families was somewhat higher.

Black family incomes in the urban north were substantially higher than those of black southern families, although the differential in northern and southern white families was much smaller.[6]

Prior to 1930, numerous blacks worked in the paper and pulp industry, which paid well for many years. However, when employees in that industry first organized unions, they refused to accept less skilled wood yard and pulp mill workers (a large percentage of which were blacks) for membership. When they later accepted them, they did so under restricted rules which prohibited such less skilled workers from holding office.[7]

Except for the trowel trades, bricklaying, plastering, and cement work, as well as carpentry and blacksmithing, which were dominated by black bondsmen since slavery, blacks were excluded from such skill trades as plumbers and electricians. Aside from these exceptions, between 1920 and 1930, only 3 percent of paper pulp mill industry employees were black. By 1940, blacks only constituted 4 percent of the industry and even then, they were primarily janitors and laborers. Blacks were usually singled out for such jobs as cooks, helpers, and the hot, dirty and difficult jobs of cleaning boilers.[8]

As late as 1960–61, the annual average income of black families in the urban United States was $3,840, compared with $6,169 for white families. Total expenditures for consumption of black families during the same period was $3,707 and $5,609, for whites. Black families expended nearly the same amount of money as white families for food, shelter, light, refrigeration, water, clothing, medical care and miscellaneous.[9]

Black and white male employment in selected occupations during 1950 (in thousands) was 3,500 blacks and 26,830 whites. During 1960, the latter figures increased to 3,644 for blacks and 39,462 for whites.[10]

However, since education bears a distinct relationship to employability, education of the population, by race, for the median years 1950 and 1960 shows blacks had 7.3 years and whites 10.1 years of schooling in 1950 and blacks had 8.6 years and whites had 11.0 years of schooling in 1960.

In 1950 the ratio of blacks with one to three years of college to whites was 3 to 8. In 1960 four blacks and nine whites per hundred had one to three years of college.[11]

According to these data, it is quite apparent that as late as 1960 black urban families earned just a little more than half of the income earned by white urban families at a time when the blacks had several grade levels less formal education than the whites.

In the north, blacks did not work in industrial plants for many years because their employment in such all-white plants would be met with active resistance of white workers. If blacks were employed in lower level positions, their promotion to higher positions would induce great resentment and resistance by whites. An employer invited a risk of disruption in orderly production if it employed blacks under such circumstances. Consequently, exclusionary hiring policies evolved which systematically excluded black employees from some entire industries. So successful were such discriminatory policies that vocational guidance counselors often advised black youths not to enroll in courses for occupations from which they were excluded in the job market. In any event, without vocational training, an applicant for a skilled position would be told he did not have the prerequisites for apprenticeship in various skilled jobs with plumbers, pipefitters, sheetmetal workers, electricians, iron workers and operating engineers. [12]

American trade unions contributed substantially to patterns of racial discrimination in employment nationally. Historically, such discrimination was initially implemented by excluding blacks and other minorities from union membership. When unions later admitted them to membership, they were excluded from holding office and restricted to menial job classifications—unskilled or semi-skilled. Although the discriminatory practices of unions have improved significantly, discrimination is still preserved at the working man's level by fundamental internal barriers. Many unions have no black executive board members. Frequently, blacks are still excluded from lucrative over-the-road driving jobs because many whites refuse to ride with them in the sleeper cabs. [13]

Job discrimination was experienced by blacks at virtually every level of the occupational, professional, and entrepreneurial segments of the American society, including jobs for the local, state, and federal governments. So rigid was the practice of excluding blacks from most of the better jobs in this society, that "help-wanted" advertisements for jobs in most of the country's newspapers specified for "white," "colored," or "Negro." While this was blatant racial discrimination, it had two beneficial features. First, it saved the time of the "help-wanted" employer from seeing and refusing employment to a black jobseeker whom he was not going to hire in the first place. Second, it spared blacks the inconvenience and expenditure of energy, time, and money for transportation or use of a public telephone, pursuing a job that they would not have obtained under any circumstances.

Prior to World War II, even the few blacks employed by the three branches of the federal government were employed in lower level jobs such as clerks, messengers, cafeteria workers, guards, chauffeurs, and custodians. Perhaps the best employment available for blacks in the federal government was a job for the United States Post Office. For many years prior and subsequent to World War II the Post Office represented the most viable and substantial employment for college-educated black males. Many of them were able to send their children to college and acquire a middle-class standard of living. Consequently, the Post Office in most communities where blacks lived employed a substantial number of black high school and college graduates, and it was often considered the economic salvation for many a black family.

Prior to 1948, clerical employment for black women or men in the private sector was extremely acute. With very few exceptions, black women with secretarial and bookkeeping training and experience had little opportunity for employment outside the black business and professional community. Their job opportunities in the private sector were so limited that many of them with such training and experience left their homes in the several states to assume employment in entry-level positions of federal agencies in Washington, D.C., during and subsequent to World War II. Many eagerly went to Washington in such numbers that a dormitory facility known as Slowe Hall near the Howard University campus was provided to accommodate their job-commuting arrangement.

It was not until late 1949–50 that the lily-white insurance industry of America cracked the doors of economic opportunity for non-custodial black employees, when the largest insurance company in the world (New York's two-skyscraper Metropolitan Life Insurance Company) for the first time hired thirty or more black women for clerical positions. Black men were conspicuously absent in clerical as well as sales positions throughout the insurance industry and that remained so for several years after.

Business

Blacks having been essentially prisoners of poverty for over three centuries, it should be partially understood how so few of them were able to earn, save, raise, or inherit sufficient capital to embark upon a business venture. Of the few who did, many failed as a result of inadequate education and business know how. However, as Myrdal found, one of the major obstacles for black business persons was lack of opportunity to obtain credit. Blacks in business might have fared considerably better if they were able to secure positions in the world of finance. There were few black banks and most of them were failures prior to the establishment of national deposit insurance in the mid-1930s.[14]

Between 1904 and 1948, there were only fourteen black-owned banks in the United States and the overwhelming majority of their depositors were black. In 1957, cities with black-owned banks were Savannah, Georgia, Nashville, Tennessee, Philadelphia, Pennsylvania, Richmond, Virginia, Atlanta, Georgia, Kansas City, Kansas, Danville, Virginia, Washington, D.C., Durham, North Carolina, Houston, Texas, Memphis, Tennessee, Columbia, South Carolina, and New York.[15] There were also forty-seven black-owned insurance companies (mostly life) of which the predominant majority of policyholders were black. Prior to the 1960s, these companies issued primarily industrial policies (usually of a value of one thousand dollars to three thousand dollars) to mostly blue-collar workers, whom white companies said were a high risk for profitable insurance. Consequently, such blue-collar workers and blacks often paid a different and higher premium rate based upon their alleged high mortality rate, if they were insured at all by white companies.

Thus, while insurance was always a good investment around which whites were able to build valuable estates for their surviving families through whole and straight life policies of ten thousand dollars to one hundred thousand dollars or more, opportunities for such investments were virtually not available to blacks. Investments by blacks were largely restricted to the few who could afford savings accounts and ownership of rental real estate.

In view of the very limited economic opportunities for blacks for so many generations, young inquisitive Americans would wonder what employment opportunities were available to blacks to earn a living. As older blacks will attest, most college-educated blacks became teachers after black teachers were hired by the public school systems, and many became trained nurses. A few became ministers, physicians, dentists, pharmacists, and morticians, which provided perhaps the greatest degree of economic independence in the black community because their congregations, patients, or patrons were all black. There were many bondsmen during slavery who mastered the crafts of bricklaying, stone masonry, carpentry, plastering, paper hanging, painting, as well as those of tinners and blacksmiths. These trades were passed down several generations, with younger family members enhancing their skills with formal training in the respective occupations. As a result of such occupational inheritance, many black artisans became construction contractors of considerable affluence and dominated these trades in the south for generations into the 1960s.

Many blacks became barbers and beauticians. However, the greater lot of blacks worked as domestic servants, custodians, coachmen, and laborers, and some worked at lower-level positions in the few very heavy industries or factories which existed throughout the south.

Since Reconstruction, the first action taken by the federal government which resulted in some economic assistance to blacks, was the welfare programs of the Social Security Act passed in 1935. Although these programs were established for the benefit of the national population, of which blacks constituted only a fraction of 10 percent, it would be unrealistic and illogical to argue that a sizeable number of them were not worthy recipients of such assistance in view of their economic repression prior to the Act.

Also, since Reconstruction the next action taken by the federal government to improve the economic opportunity of blacks, came after William Hastie was designated a civilian aide to the War Department in 1940, and the advocacy of A. Phillip Randolph, that black workers be hired by industries having contracts with the government. In June 1941, President Franklin D. Roosevelt issued his proclamation against discrimination in hiring practices by establishing the Fair Employment Practice Committee (FEPC).[16] The committee was designed to try to assure everyone the right to a job regardless of race, color, religion, or national origin. The object of the committee was job discrimination primarily against Negroes and Jews in industries which worked on government contracts. It tried to reduce discrimination in employment through conciliatory efforts. In 1956, President Dwight D. Eisenhower established the Committee on Government Contracts to carry out the same objectives in essentially the same manner, and the FEPC was terminated that year. As the result of both committees, blacks and Jews were employed in significant numbers in industries with government contracts.

Similar FEPC laws were enacted in New York in 1945 and in twenty-nine states between 1945 and 1946. However, most of the state laws varied from one another in several respects. They were often called toothless laws because they provided no money remedy or criminal penalty against the discriminating employer. Most of such laws provided for investigation of a complaint of discrimination and a conciliatory effort on the part of the administrative agency to persuade the employer to abate the practice or resolve the dispute. If the employer refused to resolve the matter, the complainant was left with the option of abandoning the grievance, or instituting a lawsuit in the state courts. Job opportunities for minorities certainly increased under such legislation, but not nearly enough to eliminate a substantial part of the practice of job discrimination based upon race, color, religion, or national origin.

After considering this brief background of the economic plight of blacks, it should be clear that for nearly all of their years in this country their struggle to survive economically has been essentially one of self-help against the powerful odds of universal racial discrimination in nearly every aspect of economic endeavor. It is also noted that such employment discrimination was not imposed against blacks solely by the private business sector. Uniquely, it included the participation, acquiescence, and sometimes the legal sanctions of the local, state, and federal governments.

Housing

Shelter has been a problem for blacks since their emancipation from slavery in 1865. Initially they roamed the south, floudering from camp to camp in nearby cities and military posts. Some built shacks, others bought or rented land, and still others returned to their former masters as free workers. Without funds to obtain better shelter, many lived in the outdoors, some in deserted houses and caves or in impoverished sheds near rivers. Often their quarters had only a door for light and air and a roof that leaked when it rained. Overcrowded and exposed to the elements, many ex-slaves died from tuberculosis, smallpox, and epidemics, and black children died like flies from lack of proper diet and care.

By 1910, the black population in the north had grown to 1.6 percent of the southern and western black population—so few, that they met virtually no racial resistance. They had not yet constituted sufficient numbers to pose a competitive threat to whites and other ethnic groups for housing and jobs.[17]

Between 1920 and 1930, 615,000 blacks migrated primarily from Georgia, South Carolina, and Mississippi, mostly to the northeast and concentrated mainly in large cities. They went to the middle west, largely to Chicago and St. Louis. Forty-three thousand alone went to Chicago. They first resided in slums in black districts, then expanded from black ghettos to white slums, and sometimes, by doubling up and sharing rent, they moved to costly neighborhoods.

When whites began to feel the pressure of their arrival, some of them elected to escape the black invasion by moving to other areas. Other whites remained and fought, causing enactment of zoning laws prohibiting black occupancy. When the courts invalidated the zoning laws, they resorted to the use of restrictive covenants in wills of estates and contracts for the sale of real estate, excluding blacks from acquiring ownership of real estate, or occupancy of rental property.[18] The "covenant" utilized in such instruments were agreements between the seller and the buyer that the buyer would not sell, lease or allow a person of a certain ethnic group to buy, lease or occupy the property; and/or that the buyer would require the same condition on selling the property to another buyer. Breach of the covenant rendered the party breaching the agreement liable to damages to prior sellers.[19]

Restrictive covenants were largely characteristic of the north, rather than the south, where blacks and whites sometimes lived side-by-side, even though they had limited social contact as neighbors.

When covenants were not effective, whites resorted to force of intimidation—harassment, burning crosses, violence, stoning, shooting firearms, burning or dynamiting the property owned or occupied by blacks. After a cross-burning in Pittsburgh, Pennsylvania, in 1919, organized whites threatened to withdraw financial support of the YWCA and the Community Chest if the latter organizations did not force two black doctors and a YMCA secretary to vacate their recently bought homes. Similar and worse incidents occurred in many American cities, north and south, between 1920 and 1940.[20] The strife and violence associated with blacks moving into white neighborhoods continued nationally until 1968 when they subsided somewhat after enactment of the Federal Fair Housing Laws.

Prior to the 1930s, real-estate brokers, managers, appraisers, builders, mortgage lenders, and insurance companies operating under state laws were largely a local business enterprise. That being the case, Abrams notes, "The prejudice which has spread through American neighborhoods has been nourished by the organized real estate enterprise . . . " but which changed markedly with the advent of the New Deal—federal intervention and the coming of the Federal Housing Administration with guaranteed loans, and other federal agencies stimulating expansion in the housing and real estate enterprise. Out of expansion came powerful real estate lobbies, influencing the direction of the expansion. Some of the strongest and most effective of such lobbies were the National Association of Real Estate Brokers (NAREB), the National Association of Home Builders (NAHB), the United States Savings and Loan League (USSLL), and the National Association of Lumber Dealers (NALD).[21]

Through their lobbies and the news media, these groups brought pressure to bear on Congress, especially when it concerned low-income housing. Their influence reflected their racial philosophy which was an "anti-negro, anti-alien, and anti-anybody-who-was-different." NAREB was instrumental in causing the publication of several books on real estate. One of such books was *Principles of Real Estate Practice*, by Ernest M. Fisher. In emphasizing the importance and the character of the community in determining the value of real estate, Fisher said: "It is a matter of common observation that the purchase of property by certain racial types is very likely to diminish the value of other property in the section."

In advocating how religious and racial factors affect residential values, the book *The Appraisal of Real Estate,* by Frederick M. Babcock, included the following quote:

> Residential values are affected by racial and religious factors . . . A home utility seeks location near people . . . but always near persons of the same social standing, same race, near to churches, schools, and all phases of social life and with access to places of business and shopping . . . And so the habits, the character, the race, the movements, and the very moods of people are the ultimate factors of real estate value . . . The real factors are buying mood, hours, purchasing power, motives at the moment, directions of movements, race, occupations, religion and standards of living . . .[22]

In *Principles of Real Estate Practice,* the then General Counsel of NAREB, arguing the legality of restrictive covenants prior to the courts declaring them illegal, said:

> The individual citizen, whether he is black or white, may refuse to sell or lease property to any particular individual or class of individuals. The power of the whites to exclude the blacks from purchasing their property implies the power of the blacks to exercise the same prerogative over property which they may own. There is, therefore, no discrimination with the Civil Rights Clause of the Constitution.[23]

Until as late as 1950, the official Code of Ethics of the National Association of Real Estate Brokers contained the following canon:

> A realtor should never be instrumental in introducing into a neighborhood a character of property or occupancy of any race or nationality, . . . which will clearly be detrimental to property values in that neighborhood.[24]

The above philosophies found their way into the written official policy of government appraisals and assisted in depriving minorities of government-aided housing. Such policies assisted in establishing thousands of FHA neighborhoods inhabited by ethnically "homogenous groups who were sold the racist reasons for purchasing, to insure forever immunity from unwanted ethnic pollution."[25]

Finally, in *Real Estate Fundamentals*, by Homer Hoyt, the latter concurred with the realtors' analysis of how land values are affected by races and nationalities, from most to the least favorable, as follows:

> English, Germans, Irish, Scandinavians
> Morse Italians
> Bohemians or Czechs
> Poles
> Lithuanians
> Greeks
> Russian Jews ("lower class")
> South Italians
> Negroes
> Mexicans

Hoyt noted without verification, that such racial and national barriers disappear after all the above-named groups advance economically on the American standard of living scale, except Negroes and Mexicans.[26]

The Home Builders

Until 1948, when the Supreme Court declared restrictive covenants unconstitutional, home builders preserved the ethnic homogeneity of neighborhoods with the use of the restrictive covenant. That is, they covenanted the land with restrictions prohibiting ownership or occupancy by various ethnic groups of people (Negroes, Jews, Latins, et cetera). The builder or any of his buyers could enforce the covenant in court.

Mortgage Loans

Abrams points out that the mortgage lenders were conditioned by the same racial attitudes as the realtors and home builders. They read the same books and accepted the same rationales for ethnic homogeneity of neighborhoods. Their appraisers were allies or affiliated with the National Association of Real Estate Brokers. Hence, the lending institutions prepared, maintained, and published city maps indicating in which areas certain ethnics resided, refrained from making mortgage loans on properties in white areas to Negroes and certain other ethnic groups, and induced owners of real estate in certain sections of the city to refuse to permit Negroes, Spanish, or other minorities to move into such sections. Abrams noted that local associations were the "watchdogs" of neighborhood purity in the cities. If anyone attempted to build for minorities where they were not wanted, the mortgage companies would simply rate the area out of bounds for future loans.[27]

The above revelations explain at least in part how many credit-worthy blacks with financial means to buy, rent, or build housing, were deprived of securing better housing for many generations prior to passage of the Federal Housing Act of 1968.

Disenfranchised

As previously discussed in Chapter III, when Reconstruction ended, many states proceeded to contrive various qualifications for voter registration to assure the disqualification of recently freed blacks. Thus between 1898 and 1910 blacks were essentially disen-franchised by all except five New England states. The voter qual-ifications established included the "poll tax" (a tax levied equally upon every citizen in the jurisdiction, regardless of income diffe-rential) for ownership of property valued at least $300 and literacy and understanding tests, with the "grandfather clause" exemp-tion. The grandfather clause permitted illiterate citizens to vote if they could establish that their grandfather had voted, or other ancestors were entitled to vote during the period when blacks were non-voting slaves. Consequently, the number of blacks qual-ified to vote under the grandfather clause exception was negligible.

The poll tax and ownership of property qualifications were discriminatory qualifications against most blacks because most of them could not afford to own property or pay the tax by reason of their general state of poverty. Correspondingly, literacy and understanding tests were also discriminatory against blacks because of the higher rate of illiteracy amongst blacks as compared to whites, especially during the turn of the century. These voter qualifications effectively disenfranchised nearly all blacks. Although the grandfather clause exemption was declared unconstitutional by the Supreme Court in 1915,[28] the poll tax prevailed as an effective means of excluding blacks from voter participation until 1964, when the Twenty-fourth Amendment to the U.S. Constitution declared them illegal for voter participation in national elections. Two years later, the Supreme Court declared the poll tax illegal as a requisite for voting in state elections.[29] Literacy and understanding tests were upheld by the U.S. Supreme Court in 1898[30] and were not invalidated until the voting Rights Act Amendment of 1970.[31]

Blacks were also disenfranchised by another device known as the all-white primary. The all-white primary was a statutory creature of the southern states, wherein the state delegated the primary electoral process to an all-white committee of a political party. Since blacks could not become members of the committee or participate in the selection of the candidate, they were deprived of the right to select the candidate. The practice prevailed until 1924, when the Supreme Court declared the Texas primary unconstitutional in *Nixon* v. *Herndon*.[32] To circumvent the Supreme Court's ruling in *Nixon* v. *Herndon*, Texas contrived a device by which it delegated the function of determining who shall vote in a primary election to a political party (organization), which precluded membership and participation of blacks. In declaring this procedure discriminatory and unconstitutional in 1944, the Supreme Court concluded that since the political party was nevertheless determining who may vote in electing public officials, such action was still action by the state and therefore, unconstitutional.[33]

Another device, known as gerrymandering, was used by politicians to discriminate against one group of voters in favor of another group of voters. "Gerrymandering" is a procedure by which legislatures "divide a territorial unit into election districts in an unnatural and unfair way, for the purpose of giving one political party an election majority in a large number of districts while concentrating the voting strength of the opposition in as few districts as possible."[34] The group distinction might be purely political affiliation, ideological, religious, economic status, or racial.

When blacks were the opposition group, legislatures simply drew the district lines so as to include or exclude those portions of the black community which would augment the white district to a majority, or reduce the black community to a voting minority, regardless of the ultimate shape of the districts. The objective was easily accomplished since the black community was generally segregated and therefore, readily identifiable.

In 1962, the Supreme Court ruled that gerrymandering (unfair districting) for state legislatures could be challenged in the federal courts by aggrieved citizens. Two years later, the Supreme Court declared that congressional districts must be as equal in population as possible—*Wesberry* v. *Sanders*, 376 U.S. 1 (October 1963); and that state legislative districts must be as equal in population as possible—*Reynolds* v. *Sims*, 377 U.S. 533 (November 1963).

Justice

Prior to 1950, there were few black lawyers in the south and their practices were almost entirely limited to black clients and out-of-court settlements. In some southern communities, black lawyers were not allowed to appear in court, while in others, they made no effort to appear in court. Their clients were usually poor and their legal experience, consequently, limited.

Although black clients were generally financially limited, they assumed an even greater ordeal litigating civil or criminal proceedings because courts and juries gave more credibility to testimony of white people than to testimony of blacks. Blacks stood a better chance of getting their due if the dispute involved their property rights, rather than rights of liberty, compensatory damages, or freedom or conviction of a white person. If the complainants and defendants in a criminal proceeding were all black, considerable leniency was generally shown the defendant by the courts. This distinction in the administration of justice was premised upon the assumption of whites that blacks were lacking in morals and possessed a proclivity towards violence and disorderliness among themselves. However, courts often honored the recommendations of white citizens for acquittal or other leniency for a black defendant.

Where the offense was against whites, black defendants were more severely punished than when the offense was against blacks. Blacks were subject to a specific form of justice, which was often arbitrary and accompanied by a steep fine and/or imprisonment. Blacks knew that their credibility meant nothing to the court where the litigants were of different races.[35]

Where the offender was a white person and the victim black, the grand jury would often refuse to return an indictment. Even where an indictment was returned and the offender prosecuted, it was not uncommon for the judge or jury to render a verdict of acquittal even though the prosecutor satisfied the required quantum of proof for conviction.

Negro convicts often served longer terms and were pardoned or paroled considerably less than white convicts in comparable circumstances. Southern states did not provide separate reformatories for black juvenile offenders as they did white juvenile offenders. Black juvenile offenders were imprisoned with the hard-core adult offenders.

Prison conditions—north and south—were inferior, but southern prisons were significantly inferior to northern prisons. The segregated prison facilities for blacks were under the command of poor white wardens and guards. However, all aspects of southern justice were beginning to slowly improve in 1943 as a result of such sociological factors as industrialization, urbanization, migration, the activity of the National Association for the Advancement of Colored People, and improved education of whites and blacks. Southern justice could not be comprehended without recognizing and feeling the racial double standard in law enforcement.[36]

Perhaps no single factor influenced the preference of blacks to live north rather than south prior to 1943 than the substantially better quality of justice afforded blacks in the north.

Lynchings

Brewton Berry defines *lynching* as "involving execution by a mob, without trial and regardless of the existence of courts of law, of an individual who is suspected, convicted or accused of a violation of laws or mores."[37] The forms of execution included hanging, shooting, hanging and shooting, shooting and burning, beating, and kicking.[38]

While lynchings have not been entirely confined to southern states, nine-tenths of recorded lynchings occurred in the south and four-fifths of the victims were black.[39] States with the worst lynching records prior to 1907 were the so-called black belt states: Mississippi, Alabama, Louisiana, and Georgia.[40] According to records of the *Chicago Tribune,* between 1884 and 1900, 2,156 persons were lynched in the United States, of which 2,080 were in the south and 436 in the north. One thousand, six hundred, and seventy-eight were black, and 801 were white men. Two thousand, four hundred and sixty-five were men and 51 were women.[41]

Victims of lynchings other than blacks were Indians, Mexicans, Italians, Swiss, Japanese, Chinese, Jews, Bohemians, Filipinos, and a few white men. The three crimes with which lynch victims were most frequently accused of were murder, rape, and arson.

Accused violation (molestation, attempted or, in fact, rape) of a white woman was a principal motive for lynching, as well as the most common rationalization given by white mobs for lynching. Other incentives for lynching were:

> theft
> insulting a white man
> poisoning cattle
> writing insulting letters
> circulating radical literature
> breaching a labor contract
> organizing sharecroppers
> asking a white woman in marriage[42]
> talking to a white girl over the telephone
> protecting fugitives from posse

expressing sympathy for a mob victim
being the victor over a white man in a fight
father of a boy who jostled a white woman
stealing[43]

Lynchings reached their peak in the United States in 1892, when 235 occurred. The average of lynchings dropped from 151.1 in the 1890s to 31.2 in the 1920s, to 6 in 1946, 1 in 1947, 2 in 1948, and 3 in 1949.[44]

Perhaps the most notoriously shocking lynching of the 20th century occurred on or about August 28, 1955, in Money, Mississippi. Emmett Till, a fourteen-year-old black youth from Chicago, was visiting his uncle. Two white men came to the house at 2:00 A.M. and demanded Emmett, who was accused by a married white woman of flirting with her and "wolf whistling" at her in her country store four days earlier. Emmett's body was discovered three days later (August 31) floating upside down in the Tallahatchie River. A cotton gin fan was wired to his neck and there was a bullet hole above the right ear. His face had been battered plumb to the skull.

The husband of the white woman and his half-brother were arrested and prosecuted for the kidnaping and murder of Emmett Till. However, on September 23, 1955, an all-white jury returned a verdict of acquittal of the two men.[47]

Sometimes the volume of mob action fell short of lynching but was nonetheless brutal, often maiming. During and subsequent to World War II, numerous atrocities committed against blacks were reported in the black newspapers. Examples: On March 31, 1945, the *Pittsburgh Courier* reported that two black women had been raped in their Pullman-train compartment by two white soldiers in Hamlet, North Carolina.

On January 5, 1946, the Washington edition of the *Pittsburgh Courier* reported how James Griffin, a twenty-two-year old former Ninety-second Division staff sergeant, boarded a bus in Columbia, South Carolina, and took the only available seat beside a white woman. The woman did not protest, but the bus driver told Griffin, "Boy, your kind don't sit beside white women down here." Griffen was pulled from the bus, arrested, jailed, and beaten.

Newspapers throughout the country reported the tragic atrocity committed against a black war veteran upon his discharge from military service on February 12, 1946. Later on that day, Isaac Woodward of the Bronx, New York, was removed from an interstate bus at Batesville, South Carolina, because he was accused of being rowdy and intoxicated. Chief of police Laniar Skull met Woodward at the door of the bus and proceeded to beat him about the face and head with a blackjack before Woodward could say anything in his defense. The blows to his eyes resulted in loss of sight in both eyes.

The Department of Justice charged and prosecuted Skull in the federal court of Columbia, South Carolina, for beating and torturing Woodward in violation of a civil rights statute. The statute prohibited police and other public officials from depriving a person of rights "secured by the constitution and laws of the United States." After deliberating for fifteen minutes, an all-white jury acquitted Skull on November 6, 1946.

According to black American weekly newspapers, another such case was that of a black soldier during World War II in Darlington, South Carolina. He was reportedly attacked by several white soldiers and his eyes gouged out, allegedly for "looking at a white woman." Thereafter, the case was often referred to by black servicemen as the "Reckless Eyeballing" case.

It is readily apparent from the above data that the greater severity of court-imposed penalties, mob lynchings, and other atrocities committed against blacks by whites, whatever the provocation, were against the black male in particular. This was especially so where the provocation related to an alleged intimacy between a black male and a white female; or when acting out of hate and fear, white mobs deemed it necessary to make an example of the male victims to intimidate other blacks and augment their continued control over all blacks. After all, it was still the black male who was physically strong and perceived as posing a constant gender threat to a white-male-dominated society.

The Military

Although the nation's military services were always under the jurisdiction of the federal government, life for blacks in the military was just as infested with racial discrimination as was life in the civilian sector. This was not surprising, since the military was essentially made up of white male members of society and organizationally influenced by the large number of southern white males who made it a career for lack of employment opportunities in the civilian south. Perhaps the only significant distinction in the two lifestyles was the fact that unlike civilians, there was no immediate and voluntary escape from the impact of such discrimination for blacks in the service, such as the freedom to change jobs, occupations, neighborhoods, and cities—options open to all civilians. Consequently, blacks in the military generally had to endure and persevere under the circumstances for the duration of their term of service or risk imprisonment, dishonorable discharge, or both.

While all branches of the military services were essentially as segregated as the civilian population, racial discrimination was most acutely felt in varying degrees by blacks, depending upon their branch of the service, job and duty assignments, rank, promotion opportunities, and military justice. More often than not, in all branches of the services, blacks were generally assigned to perform the most laborious, unsanitary and health-hazard job functions, often irrespective of their individual capabilities. Frequently, their duty assignments were in the least desirable geographic locations.

Promotions (non-commissioned and commissioned officers) in all branches of military service were generally more difficult for a black than a white to achieve. Racially, promotions and life in the services were better for blacks in the branch of services in the following order:

The Army
The Navy,
and the coveted Marine Corps, which is a part of the Navy

Even obtaining a military education to enhance promotional opportunities was difficult and slow. Example: West Point Military Academy, the nation's leading military training center, was established in 1802. The first black, James W. Smith, was admitted to the academy fifteen years later in 1817, but was expelled for striking a white cadet over a name-calling incident. In 1887, Henry Flipper became the first black graduate from the academy. He was later discharged from the Army for allegedly stealing money even though he was found not guilty by Army court-martial. Also, John Whitaker attended the academy and was found tied to his bed with his face and ears mutilated. An academy discipline board declared Whitaker's wounds were self inflicted to accuse white cadets of being responsible for his condition.[47]

Charles Young graduated from the academy in 1889 and was assigned to the cavalry regiment along the Mexican border. He had acquired the rank of colonel at the turn of World War I, but was denied a Command assignment. Retired as physically unfit by the Army, he rode a horse from Ohio to Washington, D.C. to prove he was physically fit for duty. His effort was to no avail He was assigned as a military attache to Liberia where he died in 1922. Forty-nine years later, in 1936, Benjamin O. Davis, Jr., became the first black to graduate from the academy in the twentieth century. He was given the silent treatment while he was there.[47] A few years later, his father, Benjamin O. Davis, Sr., a career soldier, advanced in the ranks from private to become the first black promoted to the rank of brigadier general at the outbreak of World War II in the early forties.

There is evidence that some American racism was even transported abroad during World War II. Black soldiers first assigned to England initially understood why some townspeople stared at them with mixed curiosity and apprehension. It was because many of them had never seen blacks in the live flesh before. What they could not understand was why some of them would cross to the other side of the street as they approached them, with children sometimes hiding behind the skirts of their mothers. The black troops soon learned that the white troops had informed the townspeople that black troopers were as follows:

1. They had tails.
2. Their color was due to disease.
3. They were illiterate.
4. They carried razors and would use them on the slightest provocation.
5. "They will rape your women."

6. They were some savages picked up in Africa to perform manual labor.[48]

Interestingly, although blacks were admitted into the Navy prior to World War I, they were admitted largely as stewards' mates (maids), cooks, and commissary personnel (in food and personal supply stores) until 1942, when they were first trained to enter the seaman branch of the Navy. The seaman branch operates and maintains the naval fleets of the United States. However, even then, the great majority of blacks were utilized on naval bases to move supplies, repair equipment, and perform maintenance work rather than assigned to sea duty aboard vessels. So jealously guarded was the real Navy from black men that as late as World War II, then Secretary of the Navy Frank Knox, reportedly stated publicly that no black would ever rise above the rank of chief petty officer as long as he was Secretary of the Navy. However, the first dozen or so blacks were commissioned to the rank of ensign in the Navy in February 1944.

The Marine Corps, a branch of the Navy, was the last branch to admit blacks when it commenced to train the first black marines at Camp LeJeune, North Carolina, during the early years of World War II. Advancing the ranks to commissioned officers was a long and slow process for black marines.

Military Justice

As in civilian life, blacks in the military were often grossly shortchanged and victimized by quick justice under the auspices of military courts-martial.

Perhaps the most pervasive uncovered discriminatory miscarriage of military justice occurred during the Korean conflict, 1950–51. On July 28, 1950, black soldiers of the Twenty-fourth Infantry Regiment were involved in the task of retaking the rail and highway city of Yechon, Korea. The assignment entailed a bloody sixteen-hour battle in which members of the Third Battalion fought their way up and down mountain terrain several times in the midst of superior fighting power of the enemy. Although some entire companies were devastated and casualties were staggering, the regiment took the city which was the first significant United Nations victory during the conflict.

Notwithstanding, a large number of the black regiment was subjected to wholesale courts-martial resulting in convictions for desertion, cowardice, "misbehavior in the presence of the enemy," and other serious offenses. Lieutenant Gilbert, a black, was sentenced to death. The soldiers wrote letters requesting the assistance of the National Association for the Advancement of Colored People (NAACP).

When NAACP secretary Walter White tried to intervene, Gen. Douglas MacArthur initially refused permission for special counsel Thurgood Marshall to go to Tokyo to visit the prisoners, contending there was not the slightest evidence of racial discrimination on bases under his command. Nevertheless, MacArthur asked the NAACP to forward any evidence it had and ordered an investigation of the charges by the inspector general, stating he had no objection to the servicemen exercising their right to have special counsel represent them in the person of Marshall.

Since the men were already convicted and sentenced, Walter White sent another cable and forwarded twenty-three cases to MacArthur urging him to reconsider his decision. White also requested a conference with MacArthur, the inspector general, and Marshall. In his return cable of December 24 MacArthur said there was "no objection to such a conference." When Marshall arrived in Tokyo on January 14, 1951, MacArthur ordered that Marshall receive the fullest cooperation by all personnel under his command.[49]

Marshall talked with each convicted soldier during his thorough investigation, first in Tokyo, then in Korea. He discovered that between September 6, 1950, and late February 1951, there had been eighty-two general court-martial trials of which fifty-four were blacks, twenty-seven whites, and one Japanese. Sixty-six of the eighty-two cases were investigated by white officers and sixteen by black officers. All of the charges were approved by white officers. The entire staff of the inspector general and trial judge advocates' office was white. Sixty of the charges filed against blacks were for violation of the Seventy-fifth Article-of-War, misbehavior in the presence of the enemy (cowardice).

100

Although the command's court-martial files obtained complaints against white soldiers for sleeping while on guard duty (one within fighting range of the enemy) many were not charged with violation of the Seventy-fifth Article-of-War. Some whites who were so charged were acquitted without offering a defense.

The court-martial results of those prosecuted were:

	Negro	White
Charges withdrawn	23	2
Charges reduced to AWOL	1	0
Acquittals	4	4
Sentenced	32	2
	60	8

The sentences awarded those convicted were:

	Negro	White
Death	1	0
Natural life	15	0
50 years	1	0
25 years	2	0
20 years	3	0
15 years	1	0
10 years	7	0
5 years	2	1
3 years	0	1
	32	2

One black youngster convicted of cowardice enlisted in the service when he was fifteen and fought in the freezing, bloody war without telling anyone he was under eighteen years old. He knew he could be returned to the States as a young hero. As Marshall stated, "This coward remained in the front lines of his own free choice until he was confronted with court-martial charges." He became eighteen years old eleven days after he was interestingly convicted for being a coward.

The duration of the court-martial trials in four cases resulting in life sentences averaged from forty-two minutes to one hour. Soldiers awarded life sentences of five, ten, fifteen, or twenty years were vitually all black. These startling results were essentially caused by a combination of the accused being deprived of the right to select defense counsel of their own choice, poor and rapid preparation of the defense's case, and white commanding officers with a prejudice against blacks not wanting to command them. Many of their southern officers had told them, "I despise nigger troops. I don't want to command you or any other niggers." Another cause was the lack of effort of convicted soldiers to defend themselves because of the despair and hopelessness they acquired as a result of gross miscarriages of justice they had witnessed.

Marshall's investigation and report to General MacArthur revealed that virtually the entire staff (thousands) of MacArthur's Far East Command was white; that Japanese clerks in the canteens in Korea were told to discriminate against black servicemen when they were there on five-day leaves; that discrimination was allowed in MacArthur's headquarters, where all except three civilian clericals on his large staff were white; that MacArthur was responsible for the unbridled discrimination against black servicemen in his Far East Command; and as of the date of Marshall's report, the NAACP had secured the reversal or reduction in sentences of twenty black servicemen, and the investigation efforts had not yet been completed.

Marshall's report apprised and reminded MacArthur that black Americans had to fight for the right to fight in every war in which this nation has been engaged. While white leaders initially questioned the abilities of black service personnel in combat, they have always eventually accepted their participation in combat under pressure of necessity.[52]

This record of rigid racial segregation and invidious racial discrimination prevailed throughout the military services until Executive Order 9981 was issued by President Harry S. Truman in 1948. Once the branches of the armed services were convinced that their past racial practices were abolished, they slowly and surely have since surpassed the civilian sector of society in eliminating racial discrimination against their personnel. Although the Navy trails the other branches of service in interracial progress, former secretary of the Army Clifford Alexander said in 1984 that black men and women have fared considerably better in advancing in the ranks of the military services than they have been in climbing the corporate ladder in the civilian and private sector of the American society.

Restrained Social Progress

Reflecting upon the brief discussions in these last two chapters, one can only imagine the degree to which personal development and social progress of black Americans have been stifled as a result of the combined effects of the lawful and traditional systems of "segregation" and "discrimination." To the extent to which segregation did not totally isolate blacks from cultural intercourse with the majority society, discrimination did.

While most black males and females were subjected to invidious racial segregation and discrimination, it cannot be overlooked that the greater severity of racial contempt and vindictiveness (beatings, deprivation of liberty, and lynchings) by the white-male-dominated society, were largely vented upon black males, that white-male dominance manifests considerably less racial tolerance for black males than for black females, and that the swift and severe abusive reaction to black males has done much to intimidate or emasculate, if not destroy, many of them. Perhaps, these specific observations should be remembered by the reader when evaluating the personal development of black males, contrasted with black females, as well as the degree to which they may have affected the relationship between the two in romance and marriage.

Notes

1. Gunnar Myrdal, *An American Dilemma, The Negro Problem and Modern Democracy* (New York: Harper & Brothers, 1944).
2. Ibid., 208.
3. Ibid., 208.
4. Ibid., 208.
5. Ibid., 364.
6. Ibid., 364–65.
7. Herbert Northrop and Richard Rowan, *Negro Employment in Southern Industry* (Philadelphia: University of Pennsylvania Wharton School of Finance and Commerce, 1970), 22–23.

8. Ibid., 23–26.
9. Ploski and Brown, *The Negro Almanac* (New York: Bellweather Book Publishing Co., Inc., 1967), table 138, 382–83.
10. Ibid., table 105, 325.
11. Ibid., table 218, 534.
12. Myrdal, *An American Dilemma*, 388–90.
13. Jack Greenberg, "The Annals—Blacks and the Law," *American Academy of Political and Social Science*, 1973, 79–80.
14. Myrdal, *An American Dilemma*, 314.
15. Ploski and Brown, *The Negro Almanac*, 821.
16. Richard Kluger, *Simple Justice* (New York: Random House, 1975), 219.
17. Charles Abrams, *Forbidden Neighbors* (New York: Harper & Brothers, 1955), 18–20.
18. Ibid., 81–82.
19. Ibid., 82–83.
20. Ibid.
21. Ibid., 151–52, 174.
22. Frederick M. Babcock, *The Appraisal of Real Estate* (New York: Macmillan Company, 1942), 155–56.
23. Ibid., 156.
24. Ibid., 157.
25. Abrams, *Forbidden Neighbors*, 158.
26. Ibid., 160–61.
27. Ibid., 175–76.
28. *Guinn* v. *the United States*, 238 U.S. 347 (1915).
29. *Harper* v. *Virginia Board of Election*, 383 U.S. 663. 666 (1966).
30. *Williams* v. *Mississippi*, 170 U.S. 213 (1898).
31. Greenberg, 84 *Stat.* 314 (1920), 108–09.
32. *Nixon* v. *Herndon*, 273 U.S. 563 (1924).
33. *Smith* v. *Allright*, 321 U.S. 649 (1944).
34. *Webster's Third New International Dictionary*, s.v. "gerrymandering."
35. Myrdal, *An American Dilemma*, 550–51.
36. Ibid., 555–56.
37. Brewton Berry, *Race Relations* (Boston: Houghton Mifflin Company, 1951), 166.
38. Ray Stannard Baker, *Following the Color Line* (1900; reprint Corner House Publishers, 1973), 176.
39. Berry, *Race Relations*, 169.
40. Baker, *Following the Color Line*, 176.
41. Ibid., 175.
42. Berry, *Race Relations*, 169.
43. Baker, *Following the Color Line*, 177.

44. Berry, *Race Relations*, 169.

45. Clotye Murdock Larsson, "Land of the Till Murder Revisited," *Ebony* Magazine (March 1986), 53–54.

46. *The Different Drummer—Blacks in the Military*, part 3, Box 862, New York, N.Y., produced by Juanita R. Howard, Ph.D., filmed by William Miles (video television production).

47. Ibid.

48. Walter White, *A Rising Wind* (Westport, Connecticut: Negro University Press, 1944), 16.

49. Thurgood Marshall, "Summary Justice—The Negro GI in Korea," *Crisis* (May 1951), 297–99.

50. Ibid., 303–305.

51. Ibid., 351–53.

52. Ibid., 345–55.

Six   Desegregation—
Litigation

After the turn of the century, longstanding racial hatred, segregation, and discrimination against blacks continued undaunted in
the United States until the establishment of the National Association for the Advancement of Colored People (NAACP) in New
York in 1909 by Dr. W. E. B. Dubois and fifty-nine other committed
persons, black and white. Originally, the organization worked for
the prevention of violence (lynchings) against blacks, the impos-
ition of unjust legal penalties, and job discrimination against them.
Its battlegrounds were later expanded to include lobbying for legislative enactment of anti-lynching and other laws against racial
discrimination of blacks and litigation in the courts to protect the
constitutional rights and privileges of blacks. It also became a
strong advocate and conferee with the chief executive's office of
the United States on behalf of blacks. It chartered local chapters
in many communities in the nation, but its lobby for passage of
a federal anti-lynching law was unsuccessful.

   In 1910, one year after the birth of the NAACP, the National
Urban League was established to eliminate discrimination and
enhance equal opportunities for blacks and other minorities. The
league's multi-approach to the problems is primarily educational
and social services. It urges employers to provide fair employment
opportunities for minorities, it renders tutorial assistance, guidance and counseling to students, domestic counseling to families,
and arranges for apprenticeship training and job placement. It,
also, conducts studies, collects, and maintains current statistical
data relative to education, employment, housing, families, and
an array of social problems affecting the black community.

   While both the NAACP and the National Urban League were
able to relieve discrimination in many specific and general individual situations through efforts of persuasion and reconciliation,

laws mandating racial segregation and discrimination against blacks remained intact until both systems were later legally attacked. Thus, lawsuits by blacks initiated the process of desegregation and brought about the realization of some civil rights.

The words *desegregation* and *civil rights* as used in this context do not necessarily mean total elimination of physical and social separation of the races or a blanket grant to blacks of all constitutional powers, rights, and privileges enjoyed by whites. Instead, *desegregation* means the gradual abolition of all laws and policies, whether by legislative enactment, judicial decree, executive order, or business practice, that required the separation of whites and blacks under specific circumstances.

The words *civil rights* mean the judicial invalidation of laws that denied blacks the free exercise of constitutional or statutory rights, powers and privileges, or the enactment of laws prohibiting states or persons from denying blacks and other citizens the free exercise of such rights, powers, and privileges, because of color, race, religion, sex, or national origin, as well as laws providing redress for their violation.

The Birth of Desegregation—1935

Thus racial desegregation and civil rights for black Americans were not achieved easily or overnight. The process of desegregation commenced long before the initial thrust of the civil rights movement of the late 1950s and early sixties. The struggle itself was a long, protracted, expensive, agonizing, bloody, life and death, piece-meal process which continued for a duration of approximately thirty-three years—from June 1935 until enactment of the Federal Fair Housing Act in June 1968.

Conceding there may be some uncertainty or disagreement about the precise birthdate of desegregation, legal history appears to indicate that a reasonable and meaningful time frame would include the June 25, 1935, Baltimore City Court victory by the NAACP in *Murray* v. *Pearson, et al.*[1]

However, the foundation for that legal attack on de jure segregation commenced earlier, when the Amherst honor graduate and *Harvard Law Review* scholar Charles H. Houston was brought to Howard University by President Mordecai Johnson in the late 1920s, to upgrade the law school. Houston immediately proceeded to build the law faculty with such legal heavyweights as his second cousin, Amherst honor graduate and *Harvard Law Review* scholar William Hastie, Ohio State University's top law graduate, Leon Ransom, and a selection of bright and dedicated black students. These, with other highly qualified professors under Houston's leadership, began to raise the quality of instruction and scholastic standards of the law school.

By 1931, the law school was fully accredited and the professors were molding many of their black students into very able and courageous young lawyers. They urged their students to become social engineers by utilizing the courts to fight for the rights of blacks and the improvement of their general welfare as citizens. Thurgood Marshall was one of their scholarly students.

Meanwhile, the NAACP's Legal Defense Fund and part-time legal staff in New York was headed by Arthur Spingarn. One of the organization's chief concerns was the rigid racial segregation in education throughout the south, where more than 75 percent of the black population then resided. Thus, the organization retained the part-time services of the Jewish Harvard law review scholar, Nathan R. Margold, with whom Houston had worked on the law review at Harvard, to develop a strategy to legally attack segregation in public education.[2]

Two years later (1933), Margold submitted his report in which he suggested not attacking the constitutionality of segregated education—the "separate but equal" doctrine established in *Plessy* v. *Ferguson,*—but rather, to focus on showing the courts that the segregating states were not complying with *Plessy* v. *Ferguson.* That is, they were not providing equal educational facilities for blacks. The latter approach was deemed less vulnerable to defeat than the former. Both Hastie and Marshall praised the Margold report as an exceptional prescription for legal action, even though Houston later made wise and practical modifications of it.[3]

While Houston was upgrading Howard Law School in the late 1920s and early thirties, James M. Nabrit, Jr., a black scholar and alumnus of Northwestern University Law School and Texas practitioner associated with black practitioners, Carter L. Wesley and Jack Adkins, were litigating the voting rights of blacks in Texas. Their legal action was probably the first civil rights lawsuit tried by black lawyers in the country. Their case, *Nixon* v. *Herndon*, was finally argued victoriously by Margold in the U.S. Supreme Court. The fruits of the victory were rendered nil, because Texas thereafter amended its laws governing primary elections and black voters were left equally deprived of primary participation until 1944, when *Smith* v. *Allright* was decided.

Fortuitously, both Nathan Margold and Executive Secretary James Weldon Johnson departed the NAACP at nearly the same time in 1933. Walter Frances White succeeded Johnson. Almost immediately, White prevailed upon Charles Houston of Howard Law School to become the full-time special counsel to the NAACP, but Houston was still busy upgrading the law school and involved in other legal matters, including advising Walter White.

Thurgood Marshall and Oliver W. Hill graduated first and second, respectively, in the Howard law class of 1933. They, along with other Howard law graduates and their former law professors would be heard from in the near future. Later, Houston succeeded in having James Nabrit of Texas join the Howard law faculty where Nabrit organized the first civil rights law course in the nation. They were joined by Houston's cousin, *Harvard Law Review* alumnus William Hastie, and Leon Ransom, honor graduate of Ohio State University Law School. William Robert Ming, Jr., a law review graduate of the University of Chicago, later also joined the Howard law faculty and so did University of California law scholar George M. Johnson, *Harvard Law Review* scholar Herbert Reid, Harvard law scholar Charles Quick, Howard law scholar James Washington, University of Denver law scholar Howard Jenkins, Jr., Howard law scholar Frank Reeves, and Harvard law scholar Charles Duncan. These and other black legal scholars made significant improvement in the quality of instruction and scholarship of the law students. Howard Law School became a "living laboratory where civil rights law was invented by team work."[4]

Meanwhile, since early 1933, nine blacks had been denied admission to the University of Maryland Law School in Baltimore. The Washington, D.C. Chapter (Mu Lambda) of the black Alpha

Phi Alpha Fraternity and its assistant legal counsel, Belford V. Lawson, were contemplating a lawsuit to compel admission of blacks to the University of Maryland. Thurgood Marshall was practicing in Baltimore at the time and had been collaborating with Houston since 1934. Marshall was aware of the problem and the plans of the Washington Chapter of the Alpha Phi Alpha Fraternity, a national organization of which both Marshall and Houston were members. Marshall apprised Houston of the Washington litigation plan. After considerable deliberation by Houston, the NAACP filed the suit of *Murray v. Pearson, et al.*, in the spring of 1935. Donald Murray, a recent graduate of Dartmouth College was denied admission to the Maryland Law School by University officials because he was black. Unlike most other segregating states, neither Maryland's constitution nor its statutes prohibited blacks from attending its state university.

Although state law provided for blacks to attend black state colleges and for them to attend graduate schools elsewhere, the Maryland legislature had not appropriated funds for such out-of-state expenses. Since there was no separate law school for blacks in the state and the state had not made appropriation for blacks to attend law or graduate schools outside the state, the court, on June 25, 1935, ordered Murray's admission to the university's law school. The court said that denying Murray admission constituted a denial of equal protection under the law, and in January 1936, the State's highest court affirmed the decision.

The Murray decision represents the first significant civil rights court decision won by Charles Houston, who tried the case for the NAACP with the assistance of Marshall. However, the decision rendered by the Maryland Supreme Court was effective only within the state of Maryland, while segregation in higher education remained alive and well in other segregating states.[5]

After the Murray victory in June 1935, Houston accepted Walter White's offer and became special counsel for the NAACP's Legal Defense Fund in New York.[6] Between 1935 and 1936, Thurgood Marshall was busy in Maryland urging black teachers to fight for equalization of salaries of white and black teachers. Marshall joined Houston at the Fund in New York in 1936,[7] where he continued to profit from Houston's tutelage. At that time, Houston was collaborating with Marshall and other black lawyers on the spade work for legal action for the equalization of teachers' salaries in Maryland and Virginia, and the case of Lloyd Gaines, a black applicant for admission to the University of Missouri Law School. The approach was in keeping with Houston's modification of the Margold plan. Instead of attacking segregation in elementary and secondary schools, as Margold outlined, the attack was initiated at the graduate school level, where an educated black adult candidate would probably be considered less objectionable by whites, and white resistance less intense in border states like Missouri.

In the *Gaines* case, the plaintiff, Lloyd Gaines, was a black male graduate of Lincoln University, a university for blacks, in Jefferson City, Missouri. He applied for admission to the University of Missouri Law School in Columbia, Missouri, for whites. There was no state law school for blacks. Although Gaines was qualified, he was denied admission because the constitution and by-laws of Missouri prohibited the admission of blacks to the University of Missouri. Gaines was, therefore, referred to the president of Lincoln University and advised by the Missouri University's Registrar to examine a state statute which provided for blacks to attend a law school in an adjacent state—tuition fee to be paid by Missouri, pending full development of a law school at Lincoln for blacks.

With the assistance of the NAACP and the distinguished black legal scholar Charles H. Houston, considered by many the father and pioneer of black civil rights litigation, along with Sidney R. Redmond and Leon A. Ransom, the Gaines suit was instituted and appealed through the Missouri state courts. On final appeal to the U.S. Supreme Court, the court in a long-rationalizing opinion by Chief Justice Hughes held that Gaines was entitled to admission to the University of Missouri Law School. The court stated that Gaines' right to be admitted is a personal right, and denying his admission was a denial of the "separate but equal" interpretation of the equal protection clause of the 14th Amendment, in the absence of other and proper provision for his legal training.[8]

Implicit in the court's opinion, which frequently referred to blacks as "negroes," was but one of the many illustrations of how the court struggled to reconcile constitutional justice with the sociology of racism in the United States at the time. Nonetheless, perhaps of greater significance than the December 1938 court victory was the fate of Lloyd Gaines. His case and his picture had been extensively publicized in the news media. The NAACP and its legal staff were awaiting with great anxiety Gaines' attendance at the Missouri Law School in September 1939. Unfortunately, Gaines' whereabouts in September was unknown. He left his home in St. Louis, Missouri during the summer of 1939 in search of work.

In early March 1939, Gaines was living at the Alpha Phi Alpha Fraternity House on South Park, Chicago, Illinois. Reportedly, he went out one cold evening in early March to purchase some stamps. He did not return and was not seen or heard from as late as May 1951 and probably will never be seen again. His untimely and mysterious disappearance was of grave concern and disappointment to the NAACP, and all concerned Americans were left perplexed about his whereabouts. Speculation concerning his fate included foul play by hoodlums, his receipt of a bribe not to appear, having weakened under pressure, or yielded to threats from the Ku Klux Klan, and his escape to a foreign country living under an assumed name. None of these and other speculative rumors were ever verified. Since Gaines could not be found, he was not available to attend the Missouri Law School in the fall of 1939. However, his Supreme Court victory established a legal precedent, which made it easier for other state resident blacks to gain admission to the University of Missouri, and for black residents in other states to be admitted to their state university and pursue courses of study not otherwise available to taxpaying blacks in segregating states other than Maryland.[9]

Houston left the Defense Fund in April 1938 and returned to Washington, D.C. to rebuild his law firm and further transform Howard Law School into a first-rate law school and citadel for civil rights legal training. However, his counsel and services remained available to the fund.[10]

Equalization of Pay for Teachers—1940

Marshall succeeded Houston as Special Counsel for the Fund,[11] and in November 1939, won his first civil rights case before the U.S. District Court for equalization of teachers' salaries in Maryland.[12] Thereafter, the fund's legal battlefront shifted to Virginia.

Norfolk, Virginia, like virtually all southern states, counties, and cities, maintained over a long period of years a policy and practice of paying black public school teachers and principals less salary than white teachers and principals with the same qualifications, certificates, and experience for performing the same duties and services.

Melvin O. Alston, a black teacher with the necessary certification for all teachers, was being paid an annual salary of $921, as compared with $1,200 for his white male counterpart. The Norfolk salary scale for white and black public school teachers was as follows[*]:

	Salaries now being paid teachers new to the system	Maximum salary being paid (affecting only those in system before increment plan was discontinued)
Negro		
Elementary Normal		$960.00
Certificate	$597.50	960.00
Degree	611.00	960.00
High School		1,105.20
Women	699.00	1,235.00
Men	784.50	1,235.00
White		
Elementary Normal		
Certificate	850.00	1,425.00
Degree	937.00	1,425.00
High School		
Women	970.00	1,900.00
Men	1,200.00	2,185.00

Federal Reporter (F2d).

Alston and the all-black Norfolk Teachers Association instituted suit in the U.S. District Court to declare the salary differential unconstitutional and to restrain the practice by the city. The district court dismissed the suit on the ground that Alston had waived his constitutional right to be paid a salary equal to that of whites by having signed a contract to teach at the lesser fixed rate in the contract.

On appeal to the U.S. Court of Appeals, Alston was represented by Thurgood Marshall, William H. Hastie, and Marshall's law classmate, Oliver W. Hill, of Richmond, Virginia.

In reversing the district court, the court of appeals held that the city's salary differential for black and white teachers denied Alston the equal protection of the laws; that Alston was not precluded from seeking relief by the mere fact that he had signed a contract with the school board at a fixed rate; and that in granting a citizen a privilege to teach, a city cannot impose a condition that he relinquish his constitutional right to equal protection of the law. [13]

Similar lawsuits were subsequently instituted and litigated with success in several of the southern states for equalization of salaries of black and white teachers. The Defense Fund was involved in those and numerous other civil and criminal cases not cited or discussed in this chapter. However, the additional cases cited and discussed below are discussed because they show when the courts began to enforce or clarify constitutional rights of blacks. They all illustrate the intensity of the resistance by states and entrepreneurs to comply with the supreme law of the land (in providing separate but equal facilities) as previously declared by the Supreme Court in *Plessy* v. *Ferguson* (1896).

Pullman Train Coaches— April 1941

Although few blacks were financially able, or had reason to purchase first-class train services in Pullman coaches in the 1930s, the few who might have, undoubtedly were denied their accommodations because of their race.

In 1937, Arthur W. Mitchell of Chicago, Illinois, was the only black member in the U.S. Congress. He purchased a round-trip ticket and boarded a train in Chicago on the afternoon of April 20, 1937. His destination was Hot Springs, Arkansas. He requested a bedroom, but since none was available he was provided a sleeper for which he paid the fare of ninety cents. After the train left Tennessee and was crossing the Mississippi river into Arkansas, the white conductor collected his Hot Springs ticket, but refused to accept his ticket for the Pullman seat; he protested and refused to move to the coach seats provided for blacks, in compliance with the carrier's rules and Arkansas segregation laws. The conductor offered him a refund of his first-class ticket, but Mitchell did not claim the refund. Upon threat of arrest, Representative Mitchell transferred to an ill-equipped second-class coach compartment reserved for black women.

Subsequently, Congressman Mitchell filed a complaint against the railway company with the Interstate Commerce Commission, which regulates railway companies engaged in interstate travel. The complaint charged unlawful discrimination in the quality of the facilities afforded him. The commission dismissed the complaint on the grounds that the company's policy and the Arkansas separate-coach law applied to Mitchell even though he was an interstate passenger. Mitchell appealed the dismissal all the way to the U.S. Supreme Court.

In reversing the lower Court on April 28, 1941, the Supreme Court remanded the case to the U.S. District Court with directions to set aside the commission's dismissal order because the railway company, as a common carrier, was prohibited by the Interstate Commerce Act from subjecting "any person . . . to undue or unreasonable prejudice or disadvantage in any respect whatsoever" and that such discrimination against Mitchell also denied him the equal protection of the law (separate-but-equal sleeping facilities) in violation of the Fourteenth Amendment to the Constitution.[14]

Brushfire litigation by the Defense Fund continued in segregating states during the war years (1941–45) while Marshall expanded the legal staff of the Fund with very bright and able lawyers in preparation for the major battles to come. Howard law graduate Robert L. Carter (black) was hired in 1945, Fordham law graduate Franklin Williams (black) in 1945, Brooklyn College law graduate Marian W. Perry (white) in 1945, and Columbia law graduate Constance Motley (black) in 1948. Columbia law graduate Jack

116

Greenberg (Jewish) was hired in 1949. He succeeded Marshall in 1961 as special counsel, and boosted his tenure with the Fund to at least 30 years.[15] The Fund was, therefore, staffed with highly qualified legal personnel to manage the significant cases instituted almost simultaneously with their arrival.

Interstate Bus Passengers— June 1946

At one time or another all southern states enacted laws which required the separation of white and black passengers on common carriers. Interstate common carriers cooperated with such laws and some carriers promulgated their own rules to implement compliance with the law.

As late as the 1940s, Virginia law required the racial separation of intrastate and interstate motor passengers on public carriers. The law authorized the bus driver to assign and reassign passenger seating so as to keep the races separated. Failure of the driver to do so or failure of any passenger to comply with the driver's assignment constituted a misdemeanor punishable by a fine of five to twenty-five dollars.

On July 16, 1944, Irene Morgan, a black female passenger was traveling by bus from Gloucester County, Virginia, through the District of Columbia to Baltimore, Maryland. There were white and black passengers aboard. Pursuant to the Virginia law, the bus driver requested Morgan to move to a seat in the rear of the bus among other black passengers to accommodate the seating of a white passenger. When Morgan refused to move, she was arrested, tried, and convicted for violating the Virginia law. Her conviction was affirmed by the Supreme Court of Appeals of Virginia.

On appeal to the U.S. Supreme Court, the case was argued on March 27, 1946 by William H. Hastie and Thurgood Marshall, with Leon Ransom on the brief. In reversing the Virginia Supreme Court of Appeals on June 3, 1946, the Supreme Court declared the Virginia statute invalid as an undue burden upon interstate commerce to protect national travel.[16]

It is apparent from a reading of only these few court cases, how time-consuming and expensive it was for a black instituting a lawsuit and exhausting several levels of administrative and/or court appeals to obtain legal finality of a constitutional right. Unfortunately, even after such legal victories, some litigants would have to resort to contempt of court or injunction proceedings to compel the segregating state or common carrier to comply with the ruling of the Supreme Court.

Additionally, it was not at all uncommon for the state against which a judgment had been rendered to resort to amendment of laws, rules, or other procedures to circumvent the Court's ruling. Such was the case in *Wrighten* v. *Board of Trustees of the University of South Carolina*.[17]

While several of these higher education cases were on their way through the appeals process, William Hastie was on the staff of the Office of the Solicitor, U.S. Department of Interior. He later became the first black appointed to a federal judgeship when he was appointed to the U.S. District Court in the Virgin Islands in 1947.[18] Hastie subsequently left his federal judgeship to become dean of Howard Law School.

John W. Wrighten, a black graduate of South Carolina State College for blacks, filed suit in the U.S. District Court to compel his admission to the University of South Carolina Law School for whites. There was no law school in the state for blacks. The University denied his application in accordance with state law because he was black.

State officials testified and made assurances that a law school of equal parity with the university's law school would be established at the state college for blacks by September 1947. Relying upon their testimony, the U.S. District Court deferred a final order in the case until it was later determined in September 1947 whether a law school was established at a state college. A law school was provided at the state college for blacks, but certainly not of equal parity with the State University's law school. However, there was no appeal on the comparative quality of the two schools and Wrighten attended the make-shift school at the state college for blacks. He graduated and was later admitted to the South Carolina bar.

The Supreme Court got the first opportunity to consider the delay of a state to provide a law school as the District Court allowed South Carolina in the *Wrighten* case, when it decided

Sipuel v. *Board of Regents of the University of Oklahoma, et al.*[19] There, Ada Lois Sipuel, a qualified black female, applied for admission to the University of Oklahoma Law School. Her application was denied solely because she was black. Although the Supreme Court had already spoken on this issue in the *Gaines* case, when Sipuel applied to the state court for a writ (order) to compel her admission, her application was denied by the court and affirmed by the Oklahoma Supreme Court. Upon Appeal to the U.S. Supreme Court, Sipuel was represented by Thurgood Marshall and Amos Hall, with Frank Reeves on the brief. Briefs amicus curiae (briefs filed as friend of the court) were also filed on Sipuel's behalf.

In reversing and remanding the case to the Oklahoma Supreme Court on January 12, 1948, the Supreme Court, citing its ruling in *Gaines* and unlike the court in *Wrighten*, held that Oklahoma must provide for Sipuel's legal education just as it does for its qualified white applicants. Its failure to do so immediately denied her a separate and equal opportunity to pursue a legal education. Since Sipuel was ordered admitted to the University's law school, the NAACP still did not have an opportunity to litigate the question of equal parity of law schools. However, such an opportunity presented itself in *Sweatt* v. *Painter, et al.*[20]

In the *Sweatt* case, a Texas trial court denied Herman Sweatt an order compelling his admission to the University of Texas Law School for whites because it found the newly established law school for blacks offered him opportunities for the study of law substantially equivalent to those at the University of Texas Law School for whites. The decision was affirmed by the Texas Appeals Court and the State Supreme Court denied review.

On appeal to the U.S. Supreme Court, NAACP lawyers argued for the first time, whether the new law school at the black state college was substantially equivalent to the university's law school for whites. After a comparative analysis of the evidence of the qualitative attributes of both law schools, the Supreme Court found that the separate facilities of the law school for blacks were not equal to the opportunities and facilities of the University of Texas Law School. Thus in reversing the Texas court the Supreme Court held that Texas had not satisfied the "separate but equal" standard established by the Supreme Court's decision in *Plessy* v. *Ferguson* and therefore, Sweatt was denied the equal protection of the law requiring his admission to the University of Texas.

Partial Compliance—June 1950

Notwithstanding the Supreme Court's ruling in the *Gaines* and *Sipuel* cases involving law school admissions, G. W. McLauren, a black citizen of Oklahoma with a master's degree, applied for admission to the University of Oklahoma graduate school to pursue study for a doctorate degree in education. He was denied admission because Oklahoma statutes made it a misdemeanor "to maintain, operate, teach or attend a school" in which whites and blacks are enrolled or taught. After prevailing in the U.S. District Court that his exclusion was unconstitutional as a denial of the equal protection of the laws, McLauren was admitted to the graduate school.

However, the state having lost the decision in the District Court, the Oklahoma legislature amended its statute to permit the admission of blacks to the university to study graduate courses not available to them in black colleges with the provision that such courses shall be provided by the university with the races separated. Consequently, although McLauren was admitted to the university, he was required "to sit apart from whites at a designated table in an anteroom adjoining the classroom; to sit at a designated table on the mezzanine of the library, but not to use desks in the regular reading room; and to sit at a designated table and eat at a different time from other students in the cafeteria." McLauren appealed to the U.S. District Court to modify its order and judgment, and thereby invalidate such restrictions, but the Court denied the motion, holding that such segregation did not violate the Fourteenth Amendment.

On appeal to the U.S. Supreme Court, McLauren was represented by the NAACP in the persons of Robert L. Carter and Amos T. Hall, with Thurgood Marshall and Frank D. Reeves on the brief. Briefs amicus curiae were filed on behalf of McLauren by the Solicitor General of the United States, the American Federation of Teachers, the American Veterans Committee, Inc., the Congress of Industrial Organizations, the Japanese-American Citizens League, and the American Civil Liberties Union.

During the interim between the adverse District Court decision and the hearing on his appeal to the Supreme Court, McLauren's treatment by the University was altered at times. At one period of time, a rail was erected around the room in which he sat on which was a sign stating RESERVED FOR COLORED. (Such a rail was erected around black law student Jackie Shropshire at the University of Arkansas Law School in 1948.) Thereafter, McLauren was seated in the classroom, but in a row of seats specified for "colored students." He was assigned to a designated table in the library reading room and was permitted to eat at the same time as the other students, but at a table designated exclusively for him.

In reversing the District Court's ruling, the Supreme Court held on June 5, 1950, that such restrictions imposed by the state tended to impair and inhibit McLauren's "ability to study, engage in discussions, exchange views with other students, and in general, to learn his profession; and that such restrictions deprived him of his personal and present right to equal protection of the laws."[21]

By this time in the history of desegregation, if not at a considerably earlier period, the NAACP had become nationally recognized as the chief guardian of the legal rights of blacks, and the name of its chief counsel for fourteen years (Thurgood Marshall), a household word associated with it.

Train Dining Cars—June 1950

Blacks were always legally segregated in railway dining cars. On May 17, 1942, Elmer W. Henderson, a black employee of the federal government, was traveling first-class on government business by way of a southern railway from Washington, D.C., to Atlanta, Georgia, en route to Birmingham, Alabama. The train departed Washington at 2:00 P.M. The first call for dinner was announced at 5:30 P.M. while the train was traveling in Virginia. Henderson proceeded to the dining car. When he arrived there, all except one of the seats at the two tables ordinarily reserved for black diners were occupied by whites because all of the dining seats reserved for whites were occupied. The dining steward refused to seat Henderson in the vacant seat among the white diners, but offered to serve him in his Pullman seat without additional charge. Henderson declined the offer and the steward agreed to notify him when a dining space became available. Henderson was never notified or served, even though he returned to the dining car on two occasions before it closed for the evening.

Henderson filed a complaint with the Interstate Commerce Commission in October 1942, alleging violation of the same provision of the Interstate Commerce Act (ICA) that Congressman Arthur Mitchell had alleged in the previously discussed *Mitchell* v. *United States*. The commission found Henderson "had been subjected to undue or unreasonable prejudice and disadvantage," but held that "the occurrence was a casual incident brought about by the bad judgment of an employee," and it declined to issue an order regarding future practices.

The commission's ruling was twice appealed to the U.S. District Court, which twice affirmed the commission's ruling. Henderson appealed the decision to the U.S. Supreme Court. His suit was financed by Alpha Phi Alpha Fraternity of Washington, D.C., and he was represented by the distinguished Belford V. Lawson, Jr., and Jawn Sandifer, with several lawyers on the brief and briefs amicus curiae filed on his behalf by Robert L. Carter and Thurgood Marshall and several civil rights organizations.

In reversing and remanding the case of the U.S. District Court, the Supreme Court noted that the one unoccupied diner seat would have been available to Henderson had he been white. Thus, it held that the case was controlled by the previously discussed *Mitchell* v. *The United States*, because denying Henderson the one available dining seat violated the Interstate Commerce Act by subjecting him to undue and unreasonable prejudice and disadvantage (discrimination).[22]

Train Coach Passengers— January 1951

For many years interstate railway common carriers (trains) complemented state laws requiring separation of blacks and whites by promulgating rules regulating the separate seating of their white and black passengers.

William C. Chance, a sixty-four-year-old black schoolteacher, purchased a round-trip ticket for travel by train from Rocky Mount, North Carolina, to Philadelphia, Pennsylvania. On his return from Philadelphia on June 25, 1948, he changed train carriers in Washington, D.C., and again, in Richmond, Virginia, to the Atlantic Coastline. There the trainman, acting on company orders, directed all white passengers in the first three coaches to go to the last two coaches, and all black passengers in the last two coaches to proceed forward to the first three coaches. Chance was sitting in one of the last two coaches and he refused to move. He was advised that it was company policy to segregate the races and if he did not comply, he would be put off the train and the police would be called.

Chance remained steadfast in his refusal to move and he was ejected from the train at the Emporia station, arrested, and charged with disorderly conduct. He had been detained forty minutes when he posted bond, was released, and continued his journey by bus. Subsequently, Chance brought suit in the U.S. District Court against the company for damages resulting from his ejection from the train because of his race and for his unlawful arrest and imprisonment.

The district court held that the company's policy of separating passengers by race was promulgated in accordance with the general sentiments of the communities through which the railroad operated and was, therefore, lawful. But the court allowed Chance to recover fifty dollars in damages for his arrest and imprisonment.

Reversing the district court, the U.S. Court of Appeals held that the case was controlled by the decision in *Morgan* v. *The United States,* because the company's separation-of-passengers policy was unlawful and repugnant to the U.S. Constitution as a burden on interstate commerce. The court specifically noted that the regulation of the carrier need not constitute legislation enacted by a state, even though the state's power was customarily invoked to enforce the private company regulation.[23]

The Supreme Court having declared unconstitutional teacher salary differentials and separation of the races by law in graduate schools, on Pullman train coaches, in train dining cars, and on interstate passenger trains and buses, Marshall and his legal colleagues commenced deliberating the feasibility and timing for attacking de jure segregation in all public schools. They fully realized they could become engaged in endless litigation throughout the south simply by trying to prove that the educational facilities for black and white children were not equal. Such facilities were not ever going to be equal.

Thus in June 1950 black Harvard law scholar William Coleman, Judge William Hastie, and Howard Law scholars Spottswood Robinson and Marshall reached a concurrence—which embraced the views of James M. Nabrit—that they would attack de jure segregation in all public schools by presenting what they called, a "two-string-bow" argument, "that at the very least these facilities are unequal and therefore unconstitutional—but equality, so long as the facilities were separate, was not equality at all." Marshall had this legal strategem approved by the Board of Directors of the NAACP, and cooperating attorneys throughout the south would proceed accordingly.[24]

One of the several suits filed in the early 1950s was *Briggs, et. al.* v. *Elliott, et. al.* This case was filed in the U.S. District Court on behalf of black elementary and high school children of Clarenden County, South Carolina. They asked the court to enjoin the enforcement of the state's constitutional and statutory requirement of separating black and white children for purposes of public education. Although the District Court found the facilities for blacks were inferior to those provided whites, it simply ordered the school district to equalize the facilities. When the Supreme Court remanded the case to the U.S. District Court several months later, the District Court held that the school district had equalized the facilities.

The suit of *Davis, et. al.* v. *County School Board of Prince Edward County, Virginia* was filed in the U.S. District Court on behalf of black high school children of Prince Edward County, Virginia, to enjoin enforcement of the state's constitution and statutory provisions requiring separation of white and black children in public schools. The court found that the physical plant, curriculum and transportation for blacks were inferior to those for whites. However, it ordered immediate equalization of the curriculum and transportation, but ordered reasonable diligence and dispatch in equalizing the physical plant.

In *Gebhart* v. *Belton*, black elementary and high school children of New Castle County, Delaware, brought suit in the Delaware State Court to enjoin enforcement of the state's constitutional and statutory provisions requiring separation of blacks and whites in public schools. The court found the school facilities for blacks inferior to those for whites and ordered the immediate admission of the black children to the white schools. The decision was affirmed by the Delaware Supreme Court, which further ordered that the school district might be able to obtain a modification of the lower court's order after equalizing the facilities (presumably to legally resegregate the children).

The case of *Brown et al.* v. *Board of Education of Topeka*[25] was filed on February 28, 1951 in the U.S. District Court on behalf of black elementary school children of Topeka, Kansas, to enjoin enforcement of a state statute which permitted, but not required, cities of more than fifteen thousand population to maintain separate schools for white and black children. The district court found such segregation had a detrimental effect upon black children but denied the injunction because it found the facilities for black and white children substantially equal.

The black children plaintiffs in all four cases—*Briggs, et al.* v. *Elliott, et al.*, *Davis, et al.* v. *County School Board of Prince Edward County, Virginia, Gebhart* v. *Belton*, and *Brown* v. *Board of Education of Topeka*—alleged that separating them from white children in public schools *denied them equal protection of the law* in violation of the Fourteenth Amendment to the U. S. Constitution. However, in *Bolling, et al* v. *Sharpe, et al*, black children plaintiffs of the District of Columbia filed suit in the U.S. District Court there, alleging that segregating them from white children in public schools *deprived them of due process of law* under the Fifth Amendment of the Constitution. The district court dismissed their complaint.

Since the first four cases presented a similar issue—whether denying the plaintiffs admission to all-white schools constituted denying citizens equal protection of the law under the Fourteenth Amendment—the Supreme Court accepted their appeals. The court also decided to consider as a manner of grace, whether the

125

children in the District of Columbia were denied due process of law under the Fifth Amendment in the case of *Bolling et al.* v. *Sharpe et al.*, and it, therefore, consolidated all five cases for argument before the court.

After all five cases were initially argued before the Supreme Court in December 1952, the court ordered reargument of the South Carolina, Kansas, Virginia, and District of Columbia cases for December 1952. In overruling *Plessy* v. *Ferguson* eighteen months later, on May 17, 1954, the court considered public education as it has developed in the light of its current function in the nation. Thus, it held that segregation of public school children solely on the basis of race, even if the physical facilities and other "tangible" factors were equal, deprived minority children of equal educational opportunities. It further found that the doctrine of "separate but equal" has no place in public education; that separate educational facilities are inherently unequal, and that such segregation is a denial of the equal protection of the laws of the States of South Carolina, Kansas, Virginia, and Delaware. However, since the District of Columbia is not a state, it held that such segregation there constituted a denial of due process of law of the Fifth Amendment, which amendment is applicable to the federal government and the District of Columbia, over which the federal government had exclusive jurisdiction.[26]

Even though the court finally came around to fulfilling its judicial responsibility in declaring de jure segregation in education unlawful in *Brown*, the court was fully aware of the problems it would encounter as a result of states resisting compliance with its decree. So cognizant of this fact was the court that it delayed legal arguments on the implementation of its decree for one year. However, even then, in 1955, when Marshall and the other civil rights lawyers requested the court to order the states to desegregate their schools "forthwith," the court in more vague and indefinite language, ordered the states to desegregate the schools "with all deliberate speed."

The District of Columbia interpreted "with all deliberate speed" to mean "immediately," and it commenced desegregating its schools during the 1955–56 school year. Other southern states took four to ten more years, with some necessitating additional injunctive or contempt of court proceedings to compel desegregation.

Nevertheless, the *Brown* decision represents the ultimate and crowning court victory of civil rights litigation because it had the most sweeping affect on racial segregation, and housed within it, patent inferences that all forms of racial segregation and discrimination were on their death bed. Hence, twenty years after the victory in *Murray* v. *Pearson, et al.* in 1935, the team of courageous lawyers, initiated by Charles Houston and spearheaded by Thurgood Marshall, and later Jack Greenberg, who succeeded him, should be truly recognized as the unsung heroes and heroines of the litigation fight for minority civil rights in the United States. Their unrelenting battle against tremendous opposition, and at times danger to themselves, did not end there (1955) but continued into and through the bloody direct action phase of the civil rights movement which followed. These great legal warriors should nevertheless be remembered with honor, alongside the brave civil rights leadership of the activistic movement of the fifties and sixties discussed in the next chapter.

Notes

1. *Pearson et al.* v. *Murray*, 182. *Atlantic Reporter*, 590.
2. Richard Kluger, *Simple Justice* (New York: Random House, 1975), 133–36.
3. Ibid., 128–36.
4. Ibid., 167, 127–28.
5. Ibid., 186–93.
6. Ibid., 139.
7. Ibid., 196–98, 214–15.
8. *Gaines* v. *Canada et al*, 305 U.S. 377 (December 12, 1938).
9. Howard T. Clayton, "The Strange Disappearance of Lloyd Gaines," *Ebony* Magazine, May 1951, pp. 28–34.
10. Kluger, *Simple Justice*, 204–05.
11. Ibid., 214.
12. Ibid., 215.
13. *Alston et al* v. *The School Board of the City of Norfolk et al.*, 112 F2d 922 (June 18, 1940).
14. *Mitchell* v. *United States*, 313 U.S. 80 (April 28, 1941).
15. Kluger, *Simple Justice*, 272–74.
16. *Morgan* v. *Virginia*, 328 U.S. 337 (June 3, 1946).

17. *Wrighten* v. *Board of Trustees, 72 Federal Supplement* 948 (July 12, 1948).

18. Kluger, *Simple Justice,* 205.

19. *Sipuel* v. *Board of Regents of the University of Oklahoma et al.,* 332 U.S. 631 (January 12, 1948).

20. *Sweatt* v. *Painter et al.,* 339 U.S. 629 (June 5, 1950).

21. *McLauren* v. *Oklahoma State Regions for Higher Education, et al.,* 339 U.S. 637 (June 5, 1950).

22. *Henderson* v. *United States,* 339 U.S. 816 (June 5, 1950).

23. *Chance* v. *Lambert et al.,* 186 F2d 879 (January 27, 1951). Argued by Martin A. Martin and Oliver Hill (Spotswood W. Robinson III on the brief).

24. Kluger, *Simple Justice,* 291–94.

25. Ibid., 395.

26. Ibid.

Seven   Desegregation—Activism and Civil Rights

The May 17 Supreme Court's decision in the *Brown* case represented the first semblance of hope for significant legal change in the status quo of blacks in the southern United States. The laws in all southern states, however, still required separation of the races on intrastate (local) public transportation and prohibited their indiscriminate use of public accommodations. Thus the *Brown* decision and prior court victories involving higher education and interstate transportation encouraged a confidence among blacks that the laws of the land were slowly beginning to recognize their rights. The patience of most blacks with the system of Jim Crow was wearing thin, and the capacity for others tolerating it, running out.

It was out of this combined climate of hope and frustration that on December 1, 1955, Rosa Parks (black), en route home from work as a seamstress in a downtown Montgomery, Alabama, department store, was pushed beyond her limit of tolerance. She refused to comply with an order of a white bus driver to get up from her seat near the front of the bus to accommodate the seating of a white male passenger. She was arrested immediately.[1] Her arrest provoked the black community of Montgomery into organizing and carrying out one of the longest and most effective bus boycotts—386 days—under the leadership of E. P. Nixon and ultimately Dr. Martin Luther King, Jr. Blacks having prevailed in the object of their boycott, Montgomery was the first, and for quite some time the only, desegregated city-bus system in the entire south. The national notoriety of the victorious boycott in January 1956 provided the first spark of encouragement among blacks that there were things they could do in concert to change the legalized oppression of segregation.

Although the *Brown* decision had clarified the legal right of blacks to attend any state institution of secondary and higher

129

learning, crowds of white students, members of the white public, and sometimes governmental officials made an effort to prevent blacks from entering school and university grounds or from attending classes. In the fall of 1956, federal and state officials clashed when Autherine Lucy, the first black admitted to the University of Alabama, was escorted to classes under armed guards. After three days Lucy withdrew from enrollment and the university remained segregated. During the next four years, a few southern secondary public school systems (including that of Washington, D.C.) undertook desegregation of their public schools. However, a number of school systems throughout the south resisted desegregation by making their first diligent effort to equalize the separate educational facilities for blacks and maintain segregation of their system in accordance with the authority of the since overruled *Plessy* v. *Ferguson* decision.

Subsequently, in 1957 Martin Luther King, Jr., and other civil rights ministers organized the Southern Christian Leadership Conference (SCLC) to work for equal rights for blacks through nonviolent means and community development programs.

When nine black students attempted to attend classes at the all-white Central High School in Little Rock, Arkansas, in September 1957, state governor Orval Faubus attempted to obstruct their attendance by ordering out the state guards. The black students were harassed, threatened, and spat upon by white hecklers. Daisy Bates, then president of the local NAACP, escorted the nine students to school under federal military guard ultimately ordered by President Dwight Eisenhower.[2]

Mass Civil Disobedience

On February 1, 1960, four black male college students in Greensboro, North Carolina, entered a variety store and sat at a lunch counter labeled FOR WHITE ONLY. They ordered coffee and were continually refused service even though they waited the entire afternoon. They returned the next day, requested service, and the drama of waiting to be served was repeated. They returned the following day, placed their order and as they waited indefinitely, they were joined by hundreds of their black college mates who picketed outside until police proceeded to arrest them en masse.[3] The Greensboro sit-in-until-you-are-served demonstration and the mass arrests that followed it triggered a chain reaction of such demonstrations in numerous cities and towns across the south. The demonstrations were in defiance of laws prohibiting whites and blacks from utilizing the same public accommodations. The Greensboro sit-in and the events that accompanied it may be said to be the spark that ignited and consumed the residue of black patience with the system of segregation. It promoted a universal spirit of pride and solidarity and created a climate in which blacks were encouraged to challenge the discriminatory racial segregation laws by which they were so long governed.

The nonviolent civil disobedience of the demonstrators throughout the south was a shock to the psyche of the white south. It was a bold assault upon the well-established legal and psychological white control of the rights and liberties of blacks. Consequently, racial tempers of the most avowed segregationists were enraged to a level of anger and hatred approximating insanity. As the peaceful demonstrators continued to picket, boycott, organize voter registration campaigns, meet, march, and sing (exercising First Amendment rights), the rage of the segregationists was translated into brutal and barbaric physical attacks upon black demonstrators and non-demonstrators, television cameramen, and white sympathizers alike.

The physical abuse meted out by law-enforcement officials and mobs against the demonstrators throughout the south involved the use of police billy clubs, police dogs, electric cattle prods, fire-fighting water hoses, firearms, and even explosives tossed into the homes of leaders or the meeting places (churches) of the movement. Not infrequently, the brutal activities of the police and unruly mobs were supplemented by some stick-and-pipe-wielding, brick-bottle-throwing segregation sympathizers amongst white spectators. Often, such atrocities took place in front of the lenses of television cameras. So profound was the impact of the media coverage of these atrocities that the conscience of white America was aroused in full view of the eyes of the onlooking world.

As the civil disobedience escalated in multiple dimensions throughout the south, some white individuals and some organized whites, mostly from the north, assumed the risk of life and personal harm to themselves, joined ranks with blacks, and became a participating part of the civil rights movement. Such white supporters often involved members of the clergy of various denominations, including Catholic nuns, students from institutions of higher learning around the country, business and professional people, movie stars, and housewives. However, as participation in the movement increased, so did white southern violent resistance. Nonetheless, the whole movement had become more organized and the peaceful marches and demonstrations overwhelmingly larger in every community of activity. Although such activity was in progress in nearly every sizeable bi-racial community of the south, the movement began to focus its time and energy in the most rigidly segregated and resisting states of Georgia, Alabama, and finally Mississippi.

The Congress of Racial Equality (CORE) was founded in 1942 by young college students to engage in what was called nonviolent sacrifice—direct action against segregation in restaurants in Chicago. The organization was headed for a long time by James Farmer.

The Student Nonviolent Coordinating Committee (SNCC) was organized in 1960. Under the leadership of John Lewis, it was an organization composed mostly of young black and white students to engage in peaceful protests and demonstrations against segregation and discrimination of blacks in the south.

As the civil rights movement gained momentum, the members and supporters of the SCLC, SNCC, and CORE assumed the more activistic roles of peacefully protesting, demonstrating, and boycotting with the assistance of some members of the NAACP and the Urban League. They also received considerable assistance from other civil rights organizations. When they were arrested and physically assaulted, it was primarily the NAACP, the recognized guardian of the rights of blacks, the American Civil Liberties Union, and a few other civil rights organizations that came to their rescue by posting bonds and providing for their legal defense.

When merchants and local government officials of a particular community were antagonized by the activism of SCLC, SNCC, and the more militant CORE, it was usually the intellectual and more conservative Urban League, that attempted to mediate and reconcile their disputes. Although black civil rights organizations spearheaded the activism of the civil rights effort, they received considerable assistance from other organizations such as the Jewish Anti-Defamation League, the B'Nai Brith, and the International Brotherhood of Sleeping Car Porters. Hardly anyone who witnessed the direct action period can earnestly reflect upon it without recalling some of the distinguished personalities who spearheaded the organizations and the movement itself.

Some of such leaders were Martin Luther King, Jr., and his wife, Coretta Scott King, of SCLC, Roy Wilkins of the NAACP, Whitney Young of the Urban League, James Farmer of CORE, and A. Phillip Randolph of the International Brotherhood of Sleeping Car Porters and the AFL-CIO. Of course, there were other well-known soldiers of the cause like Reverend Ralph Abernathy and Reverend Joseph Lowery of SCLC, the Reverend C. T. Vivien, the Reverend Fred Schuttleworth, the younger John Lewis, and Julian Bond of SNCC, and also the young Reverends Andrew Young, Jesse Jackson, and Hosea Williams of SCLC. There was also the individualistic leader like comedian Dick Gregory, whose dedication and services to many serious concerns of the movement also seasoned it with much-needed and appreciated humor.

During this era blacks closed ranks and formed the most unified front among blacks ever witnessed in American history. However, aside from the precipitous circumstances that encouraged that unification, there is probably little, if any disagreement, that no one personality contributed more to the mobilization of blacks than Dr. Martin Luther King, Jr. King was a man of extraordinary human dimensions. A scholarly intellectual and outstanding clergyman in his own right, he was also a powerful and influential speaker who invariably inspired the minds, spirits and hearts of his audiences from the barely literate to the most erudite, cold, and sophisticated prude. He manifested almost unending patience and unwavering self-discipline as he demonstrated before the eyes of the world. He proved he could turn the other cheek. He could translate Biblical passages, philosophical concepts, and social situations into language that his entire audience could understand and appreciate. For these reasons King became known as the universal communicator and the black Moses of the twentieth century.

Desegregation—Interstate Bus Terminals (December 5, 1960)

Further influencing the momentum of black activism was the December 1960 Court Decision in *Boyton* v. *Virginia*. Boyton, a black law student, was traveling by Trailway Bus from Washington, D.C., to Montgomery, Alabama. When the bus made a twenty-minute stopover at the Richmond, Virginia, terminal, Boyton entered the terminal restaurant, which was racially separated by physical designation. He ignored the racial designation and entered the section for white patrons. When the waitress asked him to move over to the section reserved for blacks, he informed her he was an interstate bus passenger, refused to move and ordered a sandwich and tea. The waitress called the assistant manager, but Boyton still refused to move. The police were called and Boyton was arrested and convicted under a Virginia statute which made it a "misdemeanor" for any person "without authority of law" to remain upon the premises of another having been forbidden to do so. He was fined ten dollars. On appeal his conviction was confirmed by the state's highest court.

Reversing the Virginia Court of Appeals, the U.S. Supreme Court held that where an interstate bus carrier makes terminal and restaurant facilities and services available to interstate passengers as a part of its transporting policy, and the terminal and restaurant having accepted or cooperated with this arrangement, racial discrimination in the use or rendition of services by the terminal or restaurant imposes a burden upon interstate commerce. It further held that such discrimination is in violation of the Interstate Commerce Act.[4]

Direct Action

In early May 1961, CORE entered upon an organized Freedom Rides Campaign to attack segregated bus terminals and restaurants in the south. The rides consisted of groups of mostly northern blacks and whites traveling by bus in defiance of racial segregation. They departed from Washington. When stops were made at southern bus terminals, the white riders went into the waiting rooms for blacks, and the black riders went into the waiting rooms reserved for whites. At a bus terminal in Georgia, a bus was fire-bombed and twelve riders were hospitalized. During the first and other rides, many riders were brutally beaten. The violence and disruption occasioned by the Freedom Rides caused President Kennedy to put pressure on the Interstate Commerce Commission (ICC) to outlaw racial segregation in terminals of all common carriers engaged in interstate travel. In the same year (1961), the ICC declared such segregation unlawful.

In the fall of 1962, a federal court ordered the admission of the first black, James Meredith, to the University of Mississippi. As federal marshalls escorted Meredith to the campus, the nation witnessed another confrontation between state and federal power when then governor Ross Barnett stood in the entrance door of the administration building to prevent Meredith from entering. The incident provoked several days of rioting during which thirty-five U.S. marshalls were shot and two public officials killed. On Meredith's next attempt, he was escorted to the campus by federal troops. Governor Barnett stepped aside only after U.S. assistant attorney general Nicholas Katzenbach presented him an order from President John F. Kennedy.[5]

In early 1963 Dr. Martin Luther King, Jr., spearheaded peaceful demonstrations in Birmingham, Alabama, the city considered the most legally segregated in the nation. For a period of six years thereafter, there were fifty Ku Klux Klan–like cross burnings without punishment of anyone.[6]

Birmingham's black leaders prepared an agenda which included the elimination of racial restrictions in stores and restaurants, non-racial hiring practices in some areas of employment, and the establishment of a bi-racial committee to negotiate additional desegregation. As blacks commenced to march, congregate, and sing, violent atrocities against them escalated in the spring of 1963, and against both black and white sympathizers in 1964. Peaceful demonstrators were arrested and many of them violently attacked.

On June 13, 1963, Medgar Evers, leader of the NAACP in Jackson, Mississippi, was shot to death as he proceeded to enter

135

his home. Bryon Beckwith (white) of Greenwood, Mississippi, was arrested and charged with the murder eleven days later. He was acquitted thirteen days later because the jury could not agree on a verdict.[7]

Since Autherine Lucy's three-day stay at the University of Alabama in 1956, no blacks were enrolled at the university until the summer of 1963. At that time, the nation witnessed another confrontation of state and federal authority over a civil rights matter. In public defiance of a federal court order for the admission to the University of Alabama of two black students, Charlene Hunter and James Hood, Governor George Wallace stood in the front door of the university's administration building to bar them from entering. Wallace stepped aside after the commanding general of the federalized national guard unit appeared with orders from President John F. Kennedy.[8]

Amidst the increasing atrocities and the rising conscience of the American people was the civil rights legislation of President John F. Kennedy's administration, pending before the Congress. In furtherance of its enactment and the violent lawlessness that beset the south, black organizations collaborated with originator, A. Phillip Randolph, and chief organizer Bayard Rustin, in organizing a massive march on Washington to end Jim Crow and demand decent housing and jobs for blacks. The March on Washington occurred on August 28, 1963, and it was the largest march ever to converge on Washington, consisting of over 200,000 citizens, including approximately 173,000 blacks and 30,000 whites,[9] rich and poor, famous and unknown, Jew and Gentile. They marched arm-locked-in-arm, singing hymns and spirituals and chanting patriotic slogans of freedom and brotherhood, as they journeyed to the Lincoln Memorial. There, they heard speakers from the several civil rights organizations, statements of support from famous movie stars, words of unity from world-renowned entertainer Josephine Baker, and finally, the ecstatic, audience-captivating "I Have A Dream" speech by the principal dynamo of the movement, Dr. Martin Luther King, Jr. Overwhelmed by his enthusiastic delivery and still in a state of childlike humbleness, the massive audience joined in singing the anthem of the nonviolent movement, "We Shall Overcome." It is doubtful there was a single person in attendance who did not believe, at least for that afternoon, that the best of America had come together, and that passage of the civil rights legislation before the Congress was assured, as indeed it eventually was. But the battle was not over and there was still much to be done.

Not quite a month later, as tensions began to ease in Birmingham, a bomb was tossed through the window of the Sixteenth Street Baptist Church on September 15, 1963, while a children's bible class was in progress. Four girls ranging in ages from eleven to fourteen were killed, and scores of other children injured. Several hours later, two other youths were slain.[10]

On November 22, 1963, President John F. Kennedy was assassinated while he and Mrs. Kennedy rode in an open limousine in Dallas, Texas. Although investigation uncovered no specific and convincing motive for his assassination, many Americans believe he was killed for his outspoken advocacy of civil rights and his sponsorship of civil rights legislation for black Americans.

After Kennedy's death, the movement was primarily focused on the deplorable deprivation of the right of blacks to register and vote and the effort to achieve that right was intensified. The principal targets of resistance for attack, from least to most, were Georgia, Alabama, and Mississippi. At that time (1963), more than 70 percent of Mississippi's whites were registered to vote as compared to less than 7 percent of blacks. The discrepancy in registration was primarily the result of generations of political oppression in denying blacks the right to vote. The Big Five of the Movement (NAACP, Urban League, SCLC, CORE, and SNCC) received the support of the Southern Regional Council in Atlanta and its adjunct, the Council on Human Relations.

In early 1964, SNCC and CORE planned a massive effort to inform, arouse, and organize blacks in Mississippi about voter registration. To meet the challenge, they organized the "Mississippi Summer Project" with the backup support of the previously organized Civil Rights Coordinating Council of Federated Organizations. The project was a voter registration campaign involving hundreds of volunteer workers from around the country to prepare and encourage blacks to register and vote.

As the battle for voting rights escalated in 1964, the National Council of Churches offered their support. The Mississippi project was an invitation to self-sacrifice, and the council established a two-week training course at Western College for Women in Oxford, Ohio. There the white and black volunteers were educated about the probable violence and intimidation to which they would be subjected, the techniques of taking a beating without retaliation and with minimum injury to themselves, and how to share living quarters sometimes with the natives of the south, most of whom were black. A sizeable number of white and black students from some of the country's most prestigious eastern and midwestern colleges and universities joined ranks with the Big Five in waging a war of demonstrations and training for voter registration of blacks throughout rural and urban Alabama and Mississippi.[11]

On June 21, 1964, project workers twenty-four-year-old Michael Schwerner (white), twenty-year-old Andrew Goodman (white), and twenty-one-year-old James Chaney (black) mysteriously disappeared. Their bodies were found on August 4, 1964, buried near Philadelphia, Mississippi. The white sheriff and deputy sheriff of Neshoba County, Mississippi, along with eighteen other white men were arrested and charged with conspiring to violate the civil rights code, and an 1870 federal statute. They could not be indicted for murder because interstate murder was not a federal crime at the time. Excluded evidence at the trial indicated that the murder had been inspired by a plot of the Ku Klux Klan. Nevertheless, the charges against nineteen of the accused defendants were dismissed December 10, 1964.

Congress, responding to the widespread civil unrest in the country, enacted the Civil Rights Act of 1964 banning discrimination in restaurants, hotels, and other places of public accommodation based upon race, color, religion, or national origin. Although the constitutionality of this provision was attacked in the courts, it was upheld as constitutional by the Supreme Court in the same year. Also in 1964, the Twenty-fourth Amendment to the U.S. Constitution prohibited the levy of a poll tax in federal elections.

Selma

With the 1964 national election behind them, blacks saw no need to continue a moratorium they had placed on demonstrations preceding the election, and they resumed their activities for voter registration in the deep south. On January 2, 1965, Dr. King told a huge church crowd of blacks in Selma, Alabama, that he would return to assist them in a march on the ballot boxes throughout the State. However, at this time in the movement, there was considerable deliberation about the older and cautious mode of operation versus the bold-crash mode of the younger people to eliminate Jim Crow in all of its forms. The young people were growing weary of the cautious nonviolent mode of action. Along with their militancy came the rise of Malcolm X, who was suspended by Elijah Muhammad from the Black Muslims Sect. Malcolm spoke with utter contempt for the white man and his unending oppression of blacks. Until he was assassinated February 20, 1965, he "embraced the orthodox Moslem faith and made a pilgrimage to Mecca."

After receiving the Nobel Peace Prize in January 1965, King, a veteran of being beaten and jailed, returned to Selma in early February as he had promised the previous month, and was arrested with thirty-three hundred other blacks. He posted bond and was released four days later.[12]

As the momentum of the campaign continued with prominent civil rights groups, including six thousand religious leaders, Selma attracted world attention. In Dallas County, blacks comprised 57 percent of the total population, but only 335 blacks were registered to vote, as compared with 9,543 whites.

On February 8, 1965, a laborer, Jimmy Lee Jackson, and ten other black persons were shot. Newsmen were beaten by state troopers. A few brave Alabama whites joined the marchers. On Sunday, March 7 (Bloody Sunday), King, joined by young boys and women, led the attempted March from Selma en route to Montgomery (U.S. route 80) through Klan-infested country to the State Capitol. Governor George Wallace previously avowed such a march would not be tolerated. The marchers were given two minutes to retreat to Selma and when they refused to do so, police released tear-gas bombs, wielded night sticks, and drove the crowd back to Selma. The incident provoked almost the entire nation in denouncing the Alabama action. Government leaders and citizens marched in northern cities to express their indignation of the incident. Religious leaders vocally protested and four hundred of them converged on Selma. Blacks appealed to the federal court to restrain Governor Wallace from interfering with the planned march.

On March 9, 1965, about 1,000 blacks, joined by 450 whites, attempted to march again. As they were stopped, they requested permission to kneel and pray and they were allowed to do so. Thereafter, they returned to Selma. White clergymen who had come to aid the campaign were attacked on the streets that night by thugs. White Unitarian minister James J. Reeb from Boston was hospitalized for multiple fractures of the skull. He later died and the indignation provoked in the north by his death was manifested by throngs of people in memorial services. A pilgrimage of whites from the north converged on Alabama. On March 15, President Johnson in a televised address to the nation announced that he was submitting to Congress two days later a drastic new voting rights bill.

On March 16, 1965, approximately six hundred students led by SNCC's James Forman, proceeded to sit down in the streets of Montgomery after they were denied permission to present a petition to Alabama governor George Wallace. In a most brutal fashion, police using clubs dispersed them, causing hospitalization of eight of the participants. State troopers in Selma used whips, clubs, and tear gas to curtail efforts of civil rights demonstrators to march to Montgomery. Similar violence against demonstrators by law enforcement personnel continued.[13]

On March 17, Alabama judge Johnson ruled on George Wallace's appeal of a lower court's decision granting the demonstrators the right to march. The court upheld the lower court's decision permitting the demonstration and ordered Governor Wallace to provide protection for them. An angry Wallace said the state would comply, but he wired President Johnson that the state could not afford the expenses of utilizing six thousand national guardsmen. On March 20, the president declared the Alabama National Guard under federal control with the assistance of the Defense Department.[14]

On the day of the Selma-to-Montgomery march, Sunday,

March 21, 1965, thirty-two hundred blacks and white supporters, students, clergymen, and others congregated at Brown Chapel. Their mission was not only for justice, but how to change the national climate. After seven miles, twenty-nine hundred marchers complied with Judge Johnson's order and turned back while three hundred continued the journey, camping three nights on the way. Soldiers accompanied them and General John Doar of the Department of Justice Civil Rights Division was on hand. When the marchers arrived at the outer city limits of Montgomery, they were met by ten thousand rested allies who came from various parts of the country. As they celebrated that night they received moral support from performances by Harry Belafonte, Leonard Bernstein, Sammy Davis, Jr., and numerous other artists. Many civil rights celebrities spoke and the evening climaxed with a moving speech by Martin Luther King, Jr.[15]

The symbolic march was achieved without bloodshed. However, Mrs. Viola Gregg Liuzzo, the white wife of a union official and mother of five children from Detroit, had marched and shuttled demonstrators in her car between Selma and Montgomery. As she was returning for another load of passengers on Thursday night, a car pulled alongside her car twenty miles out of Selma. A bullet pierced through the window and struck her in the temple. The car went off the road into a pasture and a young SCLC worker who escaped from the car, hitchhiked back to Selma and summoned police. However, by the time police arrived at the scene, Mrs. Liuzzo was dead. Sixteen hours later the FBI arrested four Ku Klux Klansmen and charged them with murder. President Johnson expressed great indignation in a televised program, and Governor Romney declared two days of mourning in the state of Michigan in recognition of the supreme sacrifice of Mrs. Liuzzo on behalf of fellow American citizens.[16] The three Klansmen tried for murder were acquitted as a result of a mistrial. They were later tried under an old law for conspiring to violate Liuzzo's civil rights. They were convicted and sentenced to a maximum of ten years' imprisonment.[17] Other white participants in the movement were shot and others injured or killed.

In July 1965, Title VII of the Civil Rights Act became effective.

It was designed to eliminate discrimination in employment. It prohibited employers from discriminating in hiring and promotion practices, and unions from discriminating in membership (Fair Employment practice). The Equal Employment Opportunity Commission (EEOC) was established to enforce the law against discrimination in employment. It provided for the cutoff of federal funds from any program or activity which permitted racial discrimination.

The voting rights provision of the Civil Rights Act of 1965 outlawed literacy tests as a requirement for voter registration, and the Supreme Court declared the poll tax in state elections unconstitutional.

In 1967, Congress established a Commission on Civil Rights to investigate evidence of denial of civil rights to any person. A Civil Rights Division was established in the Justice Department to enforce civil rights laws. Many other provisions of the Civil Rights Acts dealing with segregation in hospitals, voting rights, and employment were being enacted or becoming effective in 1966, 1967, and 1968.

As discussed in Chapter I, miscegenation statutes prohibiting marriage between the races existed in as few as one and at one time as many as twenty-nine southern and northern states for a duration of 267 years (1691–1967), when *Loving* v. *Virginia* was decided by the Supreme Court in 1967.[18]

Interestingly, the couple initiating the litigation in the Loving case were a white male and Negro female who were residents of Virginia but married in Washington, D.C., where such marriages were valid. However, the Lovings soon returned to Caroline County, Virginia, where they lived as man and wife. They were indicted, convicted, and sentenced to one year in jail for violating Virginia's anti-miscegenation statutes (leaving the state to marry interracially and returning). Their sentences were suspended for twenty-five years provided they leave the state and not return for that period of time.

The Lovings moved to Washington, D.C., and filed a motion in the Virginia trial court to vacate the judgment and set aside their sentences on the ground that the Virginia statutes violated the Fourteenth Amendment to the U.S. Constitution. When their motion had not been decided a year later, they filed a class action suit in the U.S. District Court in Virginia to declare the state's statutes unconstitutional and enjoin their enforcement. The state trial court subsequently denied their motion and the Lovings appealed to the U.S. Supreme Court. So determined were the Lovings to remain man and wife that while their appeal was pending, news reporters on national television asked Mr. Loving what was he going to do if the Supreme Court ruled against them. Mr. Loving emphatically stated, "I'm not going to leave her; I'm not going to leave her." On April 10, 1967, the Supreme Court declared the Virginia statutes, and in effect all state laws prohibiting marriages between different races, unconstitutional.

Finally, in 1968, Congress enacted a Fair Housing Law banning discrimination in the sale or rental of housing based on race, color, religion, or national origin. Other civil rights laws were enacted or became effective in the 1960s and early 1970s, refining the basic objectives of the legislative intent of the major Civil Rights Acts. Consequently, the Fair Housing Act of 1968 may be considered the last nail in the coffin of racial discrimination against blacks—by law.

Although racial segregation and discrimination continue to prevail against blacks to a lesser degree by tradition or custom, such practices are at least without their longtime sanction of law. Thus, when anyone attempts to objectively measure or evaluate the "general progress and personal development" of blacks, he or she must do so in the context of the past racial repression imposed upon them by law. The evaluator must also remain mindful of continued racial repression to which blacks are still subjected by cultural tradition.

To assist in undertaking a realistic and objective evaluation of the "social progress and personal development" of blacks, below is a checklist of the kinds and duration of past racial oppression by law to which black Americans were subjected and which they endured:

	Kinds of Oppression	Period	Duration
1.	Slavery	1619–1865	246 years and 3 months
2.	Segregation—Interstate Public Carrier Trains	1865–1951	86 years
3.	Segregation—First Class Public Common Carriers	1881–1941	60 years
4.	Segregation—Southern Restaurants	1888–1960	72 years
5.	Segregation—Southern Schools	1886–1954	68 years
6.	Segregation–Southern Higher Education	1886–1954	68 years
7.	Segregation—Prisons	1907 (approximately)–1954	47 years
8.	Segregation—Public Accommodations	1898–1964	66 years
9.	Segregation—Bus Interstate	1888–1946	58 years
10.	Disenfranchisement— South and part of North	1890–1964	74 years
11.	Less Pay for Black Teachers	Approximately 1895–1945	50 years
12.	White-Black Marriages Prohibited	1691–1967	276 years

It is interesting to note that the process of dismantling the systems of segregation and discrimination by law took approximately thirty years of successful litigation (1934–1964), and approximately thirteen years of direct action (civil disobedience and peaceful demonstrations) from 1955 to 1968, for a total of thirty-four years.

The above record is significant because nearly all Americans and most non-black foreigners have been able to enjoy nearly unhampered freedom and privileges afforded by American democracy since 1492. Blacks were the only Americans enslaved for 246 years, followed by 103 years of racial discrimination in education, employment, public accommodation, and housing and disenfranchisement by law and custom. They are the only ethnic Americans who were isolated (segregated) from the larger culture by state laws upheld and enforced by state and federal courts for approximately 329 years. Realistically, blacks have only been free from *lawful* racial oppression since 1968. At the time of this writing, they have had approximately twenty years to try to adjust to freedom unrestrained by law, and to overcome the cultural deficit occasioned by generations of their lawfully repressed educational, economic, and cultural opportunities. How well they have done may be fairly evaluated by assessing their individual and group progress in light of contemporary societal changes of the present, and residual racial repression perpetuated by custom, against the backdrop of their long and desolate past.

Notes

1. Martin Luther King, Jr., *Stride Towards Freedom* (New York: Negro Heritage Library, 1964), 32.

2. Ploski and Brown, *The Negro Almanac* (New York: Bellweather Publishing Company, 1967), 756.

3. Benjamin Muse, *The American Negro Revolution* (New York: Citadel Press, 1968), 4–5.

4. *Boyton* v. *Virginia*, 364 U.S. 454 (December 5, 1960).

5. Ploski and Brown, *The Negro Almanac*, 28.

6. Muse, *The American Negro Revolution*, 5–6.

7. Ploski and Brown, *The Negro Almanac*, 27.

8. Muse, *The American Negro Revolution*, 6–7.

9. Ibid., 1.

10. Ploski and Brown, *The Negro Almanac*, 27.

11. Muse, *The American Negro Revolution*, 138–39.

12. Ibid., 143–68.

13. Ibid., 164–69.

14. Ibid., 170–71.

15. Ibid., 171–72.

16. Ibid., 172–73.

17. Ibid., 222–23.

18. *Loving* v. *Virginia*, 87 Supreme Court, 1817.

Eight   Some Effects of Slavery and Discrimination

The detrimental effects on the lives of black Americans from generations of slavery and racial discrimination have been the subjects of numerous studies, books, and media commentaries. Some of such effects have been described as: (1) substantial poverty, (2) educational deprivation, (3) substantial family disorganization, (4) insecurity and low self-esteem, in part a result of racial stigmatization, (5) color consciousness within the family and the population in general as a result of the significance attributed to the various degrees of visible black-white interracial mixture, (6) diminished ambition, motivation, and self-confidence, especially among many black males, and (7) self-hatred—some blacks hating themselves and other blacks because of their social status, and the way they have been perceived and treated by the larger society. There are many other, real and imagined effects, too numerous and complex to adequately describe and fairly discuss in less than several written volumes.

There appears to be considerable evidence that the effects of generations of slavery and many years of racial segregation and discrimination against black Americans are not only many and varied, but probably impossible to accurately assess. This is especially true if one attempts to make such an assessment on an individual basis. Group-wise, however, the detrimental effects on the personal development and social progress of blacks can be measured best by their impact upon that basic unit of society—the family. While neither slavery nor generations of racial discrimination totally destroyed the black family, there is considerable evidence that their combined effect contributed substantially to family disorganization, conflict between black men and women over their sex roles, and restricted the social growth and progress of many family members.

146

Historical Impact on Families

Professor Andrew Billingsley observes:

The first Negroes brought to the United States were descendants of an ancient and honorable tradition of African family life. While scholars are still in considerable dispute about the relative influence of this heritage on Negro family life today . . . there is no doubt that the breakup of that tradition by the slave trade had a major impact on both the form and substance of the Negro family.[1]

The original sources of the destructive impact resulted from the diverse social norms from which the Negroes came and those to which they were unwillingly forced to adjust. They came from different tribes, many of which spoke different tribal languages. They were brought in chains without their families, often without females, to a foreign continent and culture—a coming unparalleled to the coming of any other ethnic immigrants in America.[2] As Billingsley states " . . . the slave system had a crippling effect on the establishment, maintenance, and growth of the normal patterns of family life among the Negro people. This impact was cruel in all of the Americas. It was exceedingly vicious in the United States."[3] By comparison, slaves in Latin America were treated with certain limited and specific degrees of humanity. The system encouraged the freeing of slaves. Slaveowners were often rewarded to free their slaves. Slaves could purchase their freedom and the freedom of their wives and children. They were given specific days on which they could work and earn money for themselves. A slave could gain his freedom against his master's will by performing a heroic deed for the community or by becoming a minister or having ten children.[4]

Male and Female Socialization

A brief review of black family life of slaves in America reveals that only a few masters recognized the slave family as an institution. As John Hope Franklin observed: "Frequently the blind forces of the system operated to destroy it." Premarital courtships seldom occurred. When some masters had an interest in the religious and

147

moral orientation of their slaves, they tried to influence stability in the slave family because that meant stability in his slave complement. Slaveholders did this by encouraging slaves to marry a slave from the master's slave lot. When this was unsuccessful, they sometimes purchased the slave in interest from another plantation, or sold their slave to the other slaveowner. Such slave unions often resulted in stable families, but in some instances, the couple did not learn to care for each other. Notwithstanding, this moral and religious interest of the master in the family life of slaves, often gave way to the discretionary practice of masters selling spouses, children, and other members of the slave family.

Maintaining stability in the slave family was difficult, because slave mothers were often forced into cohabitation and pregnancy by male members of the white master family. She had little time to spend with her own children and husband because her first priority was to the children of the master family. Nearly all slave women were subject to the sexual whim and caprice of white men. Nonetheless, slave mothers did what they could to stabilize their families.[5] One cannot estimate the traumatic emotional and psychological pain such circumstances must have imposed on slave husbands, fathers, brothers, and sons.

Professor Ronald Taylor noted that slavery has been considered a destructive agent in slave marriage as an institution because it subverted the relations between the sexes. That is, the system imposed responsibilities upon black women which were inconsistent with the conventional role of femininity, as opposed to masculinity, and thereby conferred on them an "unnatural" superiority over black men. Her dual role of mother/father obliterated the institutional role of father, and deprived men of a significant function in the family. The black male was, therefore, thrust into a position where conformity to masculinity was all but impossible, and consequently, he was both rewarded (relieved of responsibility) and punished for not conforming. Thus the inferior, humble, docile, and irresponsible role in which he was cast is said to have compromised his masculinity. That role to which many of them have adapted with admirable skill was nevertheless purchased at considerable psychological cost. Thus the process of emasculation that originated under slavery has been since intensified and compounded by the relations to women it imposed, "and a somewhat similar set of circumstances produced the same effects on subsequent generations of black men."[6]

While slavery had an adverse impact upon slave family stability, the immediate impact of emancipation also adversely affected family stability of freed blacks. Lerone Bennett characterized emancipation as a "Catastrophic societal crisis." "Tens of thousands of ex-slaves died of disease, privation and want." Since black males were "systematically emasculated" during slavery, they had little or no authority over their women or children, and women were not accustomed to submitting to their authority. While some women did submit, other more independent and proud women drove their men away.[7] E. Franklin Frazier noted that emancipation tended to destroy all traditional ways of thinking and action of the ex-slaves.[8]

After emancipation, the immediate priority amidst the new freedom and conjugal confusion was the concern, inquiry, and efforts of the emancipees to find other family members and loved ones from whom they were separated by sale during slavery. As they traveled dusty roads, a common question was, do you know a woman named "Sally" or a man named "Joe"?[9]

Some slaves left the plantations immediately upon learning of emancipation. Some left for a few days or weeks at a time to convince themselves that they were free, and still others, in whom submission was deeply ingrained, were reluctant to leave at all. Some freed slaves went to army camps, some to towns and cities, and others wandered about without any specific destination. The new freedom without discipline of family or master led to widespread promiscuity. Some of the moral breakdown and conjugal irresponsibility resulted in large part from the separation of husbands and wives during slavery and the disorganization which occurred subsequent to emancipation.[10] Marriage as a legal and formal relationship had not been a part of the mores of many of the ex-slaves. This does not mean, however, that many slaves did not hold their union sacred. Many of them lived a long life of fidelity to their union without sanction of state and church. When such strong relations survived slavery, the struggling effort to exist often strengthened the family bonds.[11]

All families did not disintegrate during the disruptive effects of emancipation. The black family as an institution was first established by free blacks, who bought the freedom of their family members. Many husbands worked years to acquire the money to purchase their wives and children. However, the purchase resulted in his ownership of them, and therefore, conferred authority upon him in the family he would not otherwise have had. This arrangement was the beginning of the economic subordination of women.[12]

When freed slaves were industrious and enterprising, they rented or purchased land and became small independent farm families. Also, families which had a fair degree of stability during slavery made the transition to freedom considerably easier, with the father heading the institution. However, those relations with loose ties during slavery, were often abandoned by many men who joined the great body of homeless men, who wandered about the country looking for work and new experiences. More often than not, women with or without family ties during slavery became responsible for maintaining the matriarchal (mother headed) family. The children constituting the family may have been children the mother had prior to marriage, or added after marriage, sometimes including children the mother had by a white master.[13]

Thus along with further family disorganization came an increase in promiscuity, which brought about an increase in reckless illegitimacy, leaving children of such reckless conduct in need of adequate care. In many of such cases the women carried on "the struggle for existence without the assistance of a man." It was generally by her independent struggle that she remained the dominant figure (matriarch) in the family relations. The independent self-sufficiency of these women acquired during slavery was brought through emancipation into their partially free life. Their numbers increased as other women seeking sexual gratification outside marriage found themselves victimized under like circumstances.[14] With generations of women following this pattern, the matriarch became dominantly entrenched in the social life of the black population. Sexual relations with a man were often a means of economic survival. Frequently the man was white and single or married, and the relation maintained because of economic provisions he made for the mother and children.[15]

After years of struggling with their own children, black mothers often became grandmothers, holding and exercising even more authority in the family over their own children and grand-children. After emancipation, it was generally the grandmother who salvaged and kept the generations together, even when her own grandchildren abandoned their offspring. It is for this reason that Frazier characterized the grandmother the "guardian of the generations." She was often midwife for her children as well as the children of the white family for whom she worked.[16]

Although slave families were essentially matriarchal in charac-ter, after emancipation they began to take on a more patriarchal (father headed) character. This resulted from the compelling rear-rangement of the work order after slavery. Each family generally worked a portion of the land under a contract with the white owner. Sometimes the contract was in the name of the husband alone, but in either event, it became the first opportunity for black husbands to assert authority over the family. Those males who had some schooling or training and were courageous during slav-ery were better able to assume and carry out the responsibilities of this new position. Others less capable were less successful.

However, the process by which a substantial number of black men gained a permanent position and assumed a status of author-ity in the family, resulted from the subordination of women in the economic organization of the family. That is, by husbands having purchased their wives and children, or by him having purchased land or contracted to farm land, women were subordi-nated. Men also gained authority by their participation and mem-bership in the church which was under the domination of men, where men found biblical sanction for their authority in the fam-ily.[17]

Subsequent to slavery, a combination of contemporary factors served to restrict access to economic resources and status for black men, thereby undermining their ability to perform as husband and father.[18]

Initially, while women in general were limited to certain jobs as domestic servants, seamstresses, outside launderesses, beauti-cians, and teachers, some men were able to obtain a variety of outside jobs in farming, the trade-crafts, and common laborer work which paid more money but were insufficient to support some of the large families of that era. Consequently, the education of black boys was frequently interrupted before or after graduation from elementary school to enable them to work and help support the family, including educating their sisters or female relatives of the household through high school and sometimes college. It is said that this general black family practice over several generations resulted in a significant educational and cultural disparity between black men and women, which further hindered their compatibility in courting and marital relationships.

The educational disparity between the sexes was evidently exacerbated in subsequent years by substantial family disorganization occasioned by the rise in separation and divorce. A large number of separated and divorced women were forced to assume employment and become single-family heads of household. More recently, these women and a significant number of unemployed teenaged single mothers have had the task of attempting to discipline and control growing girls and boys without any paternal assistance. Boys, more so than girls, tend to take advantage of such limited parental supervision, and manifest a decline in scholastic interest, often dropping out of grade school and limiting their education.

The following charts reflect the educational disparity between black men and women from 1940 to 1980 or 1985:

Median Years of Schooling, 1940–70

Year	Black Males High School	College (4 years)	Black Females High School	College (4 years)
1940	3.8	1.4	5.0	1.2
1950	7.1	2.0	8.9	2.3
1960	12.1	3.5	15.2	3.6
1970	22.4	6.8	24.6	5.6

SOURCE: Bicentennial Edition, Historical Statistics of the United States—*Colonial Times to 1970*, Part I., Washington, D.C. U.S. Dept. of Commerce, Bureau of Census 1976.

1980	28.3	8.4	30.0	8.3
1985	31.9	11.2	35.5	11.0

SOURCE: 1980 and 1985 data gathered from Statistical Abstract of the United States—1987, 107[th]Ed. (Washington, D.C. U.S. Dept. of Commerce, Bureau of Census).

Years Completed, 1940–80

South Black Males High School % Graduates		Median Years Completed	Black Females High School % Graduates		Median Years Completed
4.1	1940	4.5	6.3	1940	5.5
7.5	1950	5.3	9.9	1950	6.3
12.8	1960	6.3	16.4	1960	7.5
22.9	1970	8.2	25.7	1970	9.0
44.2	1980	11.1	45.4	1980	11.4

SOURCE: 1980 Census of Population: Volume 1, Characteristics of the Population. Chapter C, General Social and Economic Characteristics, Part 1, U.S. Summary, U.S. Bureau of the Census, Table 83.

The above-noted significant increase in black male high school and college graduates in and after 1950 may be attributed to the opportunity afforded black male veterans under the G.I. Bill of Rights following World War II and the Korean conflict. Those opportunities were later augmented by available college loans and affirmative action programs of the late 1960s and 1970s. However, the above charts do not show the recent and increasing disparity in the quality of scholarship of black girls over black boys, nor the consequences of the disparity resulting from black males discontinuing their education and the number of black females obtaining graduate and post-graduate degrees.

The rate of black males graduating from high school is 73 percent as compared with 79 percent for black females. Many more black males drop out of school for delinquency reasons than females. Many black girls leave as a result of teenage pregnancy. Black women constitute 60 percent of black college enrollment and 70 to 80 percent of blacks who graduate are women.[19] Consequently a large number of black women who marry or date black men often tolerate considerable incompatibility in their relations because of the scarcity of black men educationally and culturally comparable to themselves.

Compounding the educational and cultural disparity between many black males and females are the cold statistics cited by Norman Riley that: black youths (male and female) commit 51 percent of crime in America; that one out of six blacks will be arrested before age 19; that 25 percent of the income of black youths is derived from crime; and that one out of every 22 black males, and one out of every 104 black females, will be a fatality of violent crimes.[20]

According to Dr. Alvin F. Poussaint, associate professor of psychiatry at Harvard Medical School, as of 1982, black males constituted 46 percent of prison inmates. Recognizing the increasing scarcity of responsible and desirable black men, Dr. Poussaint cites Dr. Robert Staples' observation that, "if one excludes the married, homosexual and the imprisoned, there is only one acceptable black male for every five black females." Dr. Poussaint goes on to note that while a substantial number of males are not entirely free from blame for their chaotic social situation, the question, "What is wrong with Black men?" should be more appropriately reframed: "Who has wronged Black men?" He, too, suggested that the answer to both questions may be traced to their historical roots in slavery.[21]

The growing disparity in educational and personal development between the sexes makes it difficult for black males to compete to become a breadwinner or even a comparable teammate in earning the family living. Often the incompatibility resulting from such disparity becomes the source of considerable economic and social conflict, sometimes the motivating cause of separation and divorce.

As Professor Taylor noted, it is assumed that the antagonistic relationship between black men and women frequently influences the way black children are socialized. "Consequently, girls may come to hold an exaggerated view of female self-sufficiency, while boys may come to more fully appreciate their marginal status and difficulties involved in assuming a self-satisfying masculine posture."[22]

Taylor further noted that the difficulty of black boys establishing sexual identity is said to be compounded if the home becomes fatherless, since it is also said, "that boys reared in fatherless homes tend to be less responsible, less achievement oriented, and more susceptible to delinquency than other youths." They are reported to experience confusion with the roles of the sexes and are more dependent, submissive, and less mature for their age. It is assumed that they might identify too closely with the mother and manifest "ambivalence over sexual identity and overt homosexuality." Such confusion, however, is thought to be compensated for by an exaggerated form of masculinity (use of vulgarity and profane language accompanied by a show of physical and mental toughness). However, these defense mechanisms developed amongst street peers are at variance with the mainstream model of masculinity.

Other claimed defects of fatherless socialization of boys is the failure to develop a marital attitude—the ability to maintain a stable marital relationship. Anxieties arising out of their confused male status often drive black males to destructive activities (alcoholism, drugs, violence, and infidelity), causing further rejection of them by women. Excessive promiscuity is said to be a positive value of many black males, accompanied by a gratifying sense of sexual exploitation. Such male socialization is viewed as a contributing factor to the deterioration of the relationship between black males and females, causing both to harbor negative views of marriage. More specifically, many black "women are said to view men as irresponsible, exploitative, aggressive—even depraved." On the other hand, many black men tend to view black women as "domineering, untrustworthy, and often indifferent to their plight"—their confused male status, and problems of employment[23] aggravated by racism. These views of both female and male tend to poison the relationship between many of them, undermining the stability of the relationship. The more influential role exerted by black mothers in the family and her often hostile attitude toward males are likely to prevail and be transmitted to the children. Consequently, the cycle of matriarch-male emasculation and family instability repeats itself.[24]

However, Schulz maintains that the masculinity of boys growing up in a mother-headed home need not be compromised by the matrifocality (mother influence) of the mother, simply because of the absence of a father. It is not so much the lack of a father with whom boys may identify, but rather, a lack of "adequate" masculine role models that will enable them to adapt to the norms and values of the larger culture. Sometimes the mother's brothers, older sons, or her male friend may provide an adequate masculine model. When such models are not present, Schulz says, it is often the ghetto-specific "deviant" male role of the streets to which black male youths are socialized.[25]

Ulf Hannerz notes that many writers see this early sexual misidentification and confusion of mostly black boys from matrifocal families result in them adopting a compulsively masculine reaction in which they embrace a conspicuously masculine role definition. The male role definition, however, is the ghetto-specific male deviant, as an alternative to a feminine or homosexual posture. The election of this extreme male model results from an awareness on their part that they are becoming more feminine like their mother. In attempting to reject that image and compensate for it, they strive diligently to be extremely masculine. In search of a model to reidentify with, they often do not find the appropriate one.

However, as Hannerz points out, Parsons observed that black and white middle-class boys may encounter the problem of searching for an appropriate model. Since their father generally does not work at home (like Dr. Cliff Huxtable), their father's role enactment is largely unobservable, while the mother model of the female counterpart is generally at work in the home. Thus, it would appear that the mainstream household may or may not be any better a male role socialization milieu than the matrifocal household, with respect to the influence of parental presence. As Hannerz further noted in Hortense Powdermaker's *After Freedom*, the black mothers of fatherless households worked outside the home and had little time to spend with their children. Nevertheless, in spite of maternal presence or absence, some mothers have proven capable of giving their sons masculine socialization even if not to the optimum degree.[26]

In concluding, Hannerz cautions that black male ghetto-specific masculinity is not necessarily a cause or result of matrifocality. Rather, such masculinity is often a result of the ghetto male having been forced by Macrostructural factors to redefine their sexuality in a ghetto-specific way. However, such redefinition of masculinity does not necessarily mean that the ghetto male is sexually confused with femininity or homosexuality simply because his definition of masculinity differs from the mainstream definition.[27]

When one acknowledges the subjectivity of how masculinity is defined (mainstream or ghetto) by many authorities, it might be wise to question whether "industrious and responsible male behavior" should not be substituted for "masculinity," that is, economic, husband, and paternal responsibility.

Deviant Performance

Some commentators on the black family have referred to deviant role performance (behavior) of black males in the family as a reflection of a distinct institutionalized subculture of the ghetto or black community. However, Professors Seymour Parker of the University of Utah and Robert J. Kleiner of Temple University contend a more accurate interpretation of the data upon which such conclusions are based would involve the hypothesis that: "The problems encountered by the Negro male in areas of employment, housing and general social discrimination result in feelings of failure and inadequacy to perform his family role adequately."[28]

Stigmatization

Compounding all of the other problems of black male socialization is stigmatization—unfavorable branding. Doris Y. Wilkinson observes that all societies create stereotypes (myths) about other ethnic groups which serve as explanatory and valid stories about such people. Stigmatic stereotypes are diffused into the ethnic mythology through cultural indoctrination or socialization. There have been the myths about the black male's athletic and sexual superiority, as well as his psychological impotency. All of such myths have been perpetuated by social science and the mass media.[29]

Staples says stigmatic branding—an assault on black masculinity—is made "precisely because black males are black men." He further states that as one sociologist candidly described it, "Negro men have been more feared, sexually and occupationally, than Negro women . . . that the Negro man had to be destroyed as a man to protect the white world." Staples adds that "the attempt to destroy him failed but the myth of his demasculization lingers on. One can see in this myth an unmitigated fear of black male power, an unrelenting determination on the part of white America to create in fiction what it has been unable to accomplish in the empirical world."[30] Staples further states that historical literature suggests "that Jim Crow was directed more at the black male than the black female. Black women in every limited way were allowed more freedom, suffered less discrimination and provided more opportunities than black men."[31]

Staples notes that when blacks began to migrate from rural areas to the cities, black men encountered great difficulty in obtaining work unless they were skilled craftsmen (carpenters, bricklayers, et cetera). Even then, however, they were eventually squeezed out of these occupations by capitalists and coalitions of white workers. Consequently, a consistent denial of work opportunity to black men forced the black woman into the position of family provider, and the black man into the role of a supplemental helper. Economically destitute, many black families were left with no alternative to welfare, where the extremely limited assistance grant forced black men to leave their families in order for the family to retain or receive an increase in the assistance grant. When he worked to support his family, his income was often meager and insufficient to sustain the family.[32]

Growing Disparity between the Sexes

Black women have responded in a variety of ways to the plight and masculine make-up of black men. Some have accepted his prevailing image as lazy, shiftless, and irresponsible. Some women are engulfed with a memory of exploitative and painful experiences with them, as expressed in the extreme case of Alice Walker's *The Color Purple*. Other black women have been very supportive of their men. All of these attitudes of black women are understandable. As Staples also notes, "The expression of black masculinity can frequently be met with the harshest punishment white society can muster. Physical punishment, and economic deprivation, are frequently the white response to expressions of black manliness."[33]

The above socio-historical account of black family organization and black male-female socialization explains in some measure the demasculated male prototype of many black males today. However, it should be especially noted that perhaps nothing did more to compound the human waste of black females and males during the past twenty years than the substantial increase in teenage pregnancies. Child parents themselves, often having terminated their education in junior high or senior high school, are frequently found struggling in poverty and seldom able to avoid rearing children as culturally limited as themselves.

Many black and perhaps some white attorneys, clergymen, marriage counselors, and even physicians with considerable experience in domestic counseling of black couples will attest how difficult it often is to get black males to reveal their deep-seated feelings or disclose the details or the sources of their marital or family conflict. This is quite true of white males also but perhaps more so of black males. It often takes considerable skill, time, and patience to get black males to discuss such problems. As an attorney, whenever I have been successful in eliciting the cooperation of black males in this regard, they have invariably said they did not want to talk because it would not do any good; that employers, the courts, and society decidedly favored women over them. Most of them would hastily add that they believed women should be so favored, but not to the extent that they are, and not to his economic detriment. Many of them reveal a seldom-expressed feeling that they cannot compete with the sexuality of women; that women are often favored solely because of their gender, and at other times because they exercise their option to surrender their sexuality and receive a preference over males for a job, promotion, an apartment, a house or other economic or recognitional advantages. Since persons in control of such desired goals are generally men (white and black), some black men feel they are not biologically equipped to enter the competition with a black woman, and often resign or become relegated to defeat or failure by such actual or imagined competition.

In a limited way, many black husbands/fathers feel that this is still true today, and there may be some limited evidence to support their belief. One example is the application of the two-for-one principle in affirmative action—hire a black female and the employer has satisfied both the sex and race requirements of the program. A frequent or consistent application of this principle often helps to exclude from the work market qualified black males who already constitute a limited minority.

Another modality to be considered in evaluating the validity of such assertions or perceptions of some black males is the career stories of many successful black men. Many of them will relate how they encountered the harsher standards for black male progress, as well as having been a prospective or actual victim of preferential sex advantages offered black women in their stead. The significant difference, if there is one, is that they had the strategic skill to get around or overcome the exercise of such racial and sexual preferences.

As the plight and fate of numerous black men continue to worsen, the patience of black women in increasing numbers appears to be wearing thin. Many of them are becoming extremely critical of black men, if not trying to abandon them altogether. Such negative attitudes appear manifest among a growing number of black women, and even some black men, without either having a knowledge of the expert analyses by some of the authorities set forth in these few pages, including the following analysis by Staples:

> There are many black male-female conflicts which are a result of the psychological problems generated by their oppressed condition. Under a system of domestic colonialism, the oppressed peoples turned their frustrations, their wrath, towards each other rather than their oppressor. Being constantly confronted with problems of survival, blacks become more psychologically abusive towards their spouses than perhaps they would under other circumstances.[34]

Thus it is well established that a substantial amount of the social conflict between black men and women is a result of the socio-historical impact of slavery and generations of racial oppression against blacks—the black male in particular. In light of this background, it would seem urgent that all blacks become well acquainted with the historical origin of this problem and begin to

160

arrange for some informed lectures and intelligent dialogue on the subject. That is, dialogue conducted by competent and authoritative figures lecturing and moderating discussion. However, before assuming such an undertaking, perhaps both sexes will have to be prepared mentally and emotionally to participate in such dialogue. Many black males will have to be broad-shouldered enough to acknowledge that the black family has been, in large part, salvaged by black women, while many black men vented the frustrations of their social condition upon them.

Many black women, on the other hand, will have to develop an understanding of how the masculinity or responsibleness of many black men was undermined by a societal situation over which neither sex had any control. Many black women will have to be willing to purge themselves of bitterness which they may harbor from painful experiences with black males. Many black men will have to realize that most of today's industrious and achieved black women will not allow themselves to be sexually abused or economically exploited by them.

Many black women have had to assume the parental responsibilities of both mother and father. Since many of them are more educationally and culturally successful than many of their male counterparts, they have been forced to become more aggressive and dominant in their relationships with black men. Perhaps the latter pattern of personal development is natural under the circumstances. However, because they are accustomed to being the smarter and more dominant of the sexes, they must become alertly conscious of the presence and company of black men who are not typically their educational, cultural, and irresponsible subordinates. Such black men will neither docilely submit to subordination nor tolerate female domination because they are not accustomed to submissiveness. More often than not, they will simply back away gracefully.

Both sexes will have to allow the mind to be cleared and become receptive to new approaches for bettering relations between the sexes, at least for their sons and daughters, if not for themselves.

Correspondingly, the black leadership might begin to develop a national comprehensive program to culturally orient and redirect

161

many black girls and boys towards: (1) achieving a better under-standing of the nature of their divisive problems, (2) developing greater respect for each other, (3) learning to become teammates and partners and not hostile rivals or enemies, and (4) building a more compatible and stabilizing relationship with each other.

The purpose of the foregoing educational data and discussion of the origin of conjugal and sex-role conflict is to furnish some evidence of the growing cultural, educational and economic dis-parity between black males and females. More importantly, it is also to highlight the destructive impact of that disparity upon the black family—black male-female relations. It is not to suggest that all black males have been demasculated or rendered irresponsible. In fact, in spite of the extensive history of black oppression, the number of striving, successful, and high-achieving black males in the civilian and military sector today is astonishing. However, the purpose of this writing is not to focus upon these well-oriented and stable black males, but rather, upon the large segment of their unsuccessful and socially victimized male counterparts.

Nor is this discussion to suggest that all black females are responsible and matriarchal in character or that there is no room for improvement in responsibility and acculturation of many of them. Instead, the objective of this discussion is to attract national attention to the fact that too many black boys are becoming the end product of cultural waste; and that black girls are dispropor-tionately outstripping black boys in scholarship, personal develop-ment, and general achievement at astronomical rates. Thus, many black girls in increasing numbers are frequently finding themselves at the other end of the tunnel of life, searching for a comparable and eligible black mate. Needless to say, that at an ever-increasing rate, he is not there.

Similarly, the prior discussions on family disorganization are not to imply that all black families are disorganized. Again, given the extensive history of racial oppression, the numerous and in-creasing number of stable, viable, and affluent black families is astounding. Nevertheless, the concerned focus for remedial action must be directed towards salvaging the many young black people from social and psychological failure if improvement in family and black male-female relations is expected.

Hence the demand for a national, culturally redirected orientation for numerous black girls and boys is begging, even though a few positive initiatives (Concerned Black Men in Washington, D.C., Delta Sigma Theta Sorority's, and the Urban League's Teenage Pregnancy Programs and others) have been undertaken in some black communities. The longer the problem is not addressed by a nationally organized program implemented through community-based organizations, the greater the problem for single, widowed, or divorced black females to find adequate and eligible black mates for marriage or courtship and the greater the destruction of the black family as a male-female unit. Moreover, the general deterioration of black male-female relations will continue. Some insights on addressing this complex problem are discussed in the next chapter.

Notes

1. Andrew Billingsley, *Black Families in White America* (Englewood Cliffs, N.J.: Prentice-Hall, Inc., 1968), 48.

2. Ibid., 49.

3. Ibid., 68.

4. Ibid., 57.

5. John Hope Franklin, *From Slavery to Freedom*, 5th ed. (New York: Alfred A. Knopf, Inc., 1980), 147–48.

6. Doris Y. Wilkinson and Ronald L. Taylor, *The Black Male in America* (Chicago: Nelson Hall, 1977), 1–2.

7. Lerone Bennett, Jr., *Before the Mayflower: A History of the Negro in America*, rev. ed. (Chicago: Johnson Publishing Company, 1964), 188.

8. E. Franklin Frazier, *The Negro Family in the United States* (Chicago: University of Chicago Press, 1973), 73.

9. Bennett, *Before the Mayflower*, 188.

10. Frazier, *The Negro Family*, 79–82.

11. Ibid., 81–82.

12. Ibid., 135–140.

13. Ibid., 87, 89.

14. Ibid., 100–03.

15. Ibid., 103–08.

16. Ibid., 113–17.

17. Ibid., 127–34, 140.

18. Wilkinson and Taylor, *The Black Male*, 2.

19. David Hatchet, "A Conflict of Reasons and Remedies," *Crisis* 93, no. 156 (March 1986), 36.

20. Norman Riley, "Footnotes of a Culture at Risk," *Crisis* 93, no. 156 (March 1986), 24–26.

21. Alvin F. Poussaint, M.D., "What Every Black Woman Should Know About Black Men," *Ebony* Magazine (August 1982), 29. Reprinted by permission of EBONY magazine ©1982 Johnson Publishing Company, Inc.

22. Wilkinson and Taylor, *The Black Male*, 2.

23. Ibid., 3.

24. Ibid., 3.

25. David A. Schulz, *Coming Up Black: Patterns of Ghetto Socialization* (Englewood Cliffs, N.J.: Prentice-Hall, Inc., 1968), 59–87.

26. Wilkinson and Taylor, *The Black Male*, 36–40.

27. Ibid., 56–59.

28. Ibid., 115.

29. Ibid., 119–20.

30. Ibid., 134. Robert Staples, "The Myth of the Impotent Black Male," *Black Scholar*, February 1970, 6–19. For further reference see Jesse Bernard, *Marriage and Family Among Negroes* (Englewood Cliffs, N.J.: Prentice-Hall, Inc., 1966), 69.

31. Staples, "The Myth of the Impotent Black Male," 136.

32. Ibid., 136–38.

33. Ibid., 140.

34. Ibid., 140.

Nine   An Efficacy

Objectives

I hope the brief socio-historical background related in these pages has provided some enlightenment on some of the main reasons for the current general status of blacks and the many chronic problems confronting them as a large minority in the American setting. It is also hoped that it has stimulated some interest and ideas of what blacks and other Americans can do to privately assist many black families, and help accelerate the social progress of a more substantial number of them. The question is frequently asked: is there anything middle class blacks can do to enhance the progress of many other blacks? Of course there is no single approach to such an undertaking and there is always a significant role to be played by the federal, state, and local governments, public and private educational institutions, as well as the private business sector of society. However, efforts by the latter institutions in and of themselves will probably not achieve the most effective results without the leadership efforts of blacks and other interested Americans, initiating and steering a nationally coordinated efficacious program for the personal development of many young black children.

The absence of such an efficacy does not suggest that many able and dedicated black Americans are not currently engaged in some constructive efforts to address some of the many problems confronting blacks and other poor Americans. Since approximately 1980, some black local community groups and national organizations (the Urban League, NAACP, fraternities and sororities, and others) have been doing a number of very positive things to improve the quality of social orientation of young blacks. Some of them have maintained or expanded their program opportunities for family counseling, tutorial sessions, scholarships, debutante participation, recreation, or to fight substance abuse. Some have initiated programs addressing school dropouts, teenage pregnancies, salvaging young black males from criminality and self destruction, as well as other problems plaguing young blacks and stifling their personal development and general social progress. It should be recognized however, that the resources of middle-class blacks are limited because most of them are first or second-generation middle class, economics-wise. Most of them are trying to provide a decent home environment and obtain quality education for their children. Some of them are nevertheless making an extra effort to help less fortunate blacks and other poor people.

Although all such efforts by individuals and organized groups vary in their approach, scope, and effectiveness, all are apparently having some measure of success and certainly should be continued. Notwithstanding such dedicated efforts and successes, parental conflict, family disorganization, and teenage pregnancies continue to remain major problems of concern, while declining scholarship, school dropouts, unemployment, drug addiction, drug peddling, and homicide by young black males against blacks continue to loom. Accompanying many of these problems are the severely limiting effects imposed upon the education, cultural growth, economic productivity, and self sufficiency of many young black mothers, fathers, and their children.

This chaotic trend in human development is a tragedy when any American considers the increasing educational and job competition with which young people are confronted from the ever-increasing Asian and other foreign immigrant populations entering the United States. If many young blacks will have any chance at all to enter the competition, it appears that middle class blacks will have to initiate undertakings of considerably greater dimensions than current efforts provide. If they do, will they be alone in their effort? In all probability they will not.

A review of the history of slavery reveals that some of the many slaves making an effort to escape from slavery occasionally received the helping hand of white abolitionists from the north. As slavery ended, white Union soldiers and later white missionaries and workers of the Freedmen's Bureau gave much of themselves in establishing schools and providing an education for blacks. The dedication of many of them continued well into the twentieth century. When the NAACP and Urban League were organized in the first decade of this century, some whites took an organizing and leadership role in the process. After black lawyers instituted lawsuits to litigate the constitutional rights of blacks, they were supported or joined by a few white lawyers, some of whom devoted a substantial part of their legal career to the effort. When blacks took the determined initiative to desegregate public accommodations throughout the South, they were joined in that bloody struggle by many white individuals, some of whom along with many blacks, paid the supreme sacrifice. Finally, when blacks initiated a national campaign and organized the march on Washington, D.C., for civil rights in 1963, they were joined by throngs of whites of every faith from virtually every state in the nation, as well as by some white members of Congress, including presidents John F. Kennedy and Lyndon B. Johnson, who led the fight for its passage.

Thus, if middle class blacks took the initiative to design and implement an organized program for the personal development of many young blacks, whites, and other ethnic youths in the black community, there is every reason to believe that some whites and other Americans will offer substantial support of every kind to such an effort.

Should blacks be ashamed to assume such an unusual undertaking, or should they be embarrassed if they fail in their effort? In view of the brief historical background in this volume, it is very unlikely that any rational person will conceive such an undertaking unreasonable, or its failure not worth the effort. Moreover, at the rate of the decline in American morality and scholastic discipline, a similar undertaking may soon be necessary to save many American youths whose historical heritage was considerably more fortunate than American blacks.

With the history of the black family in mind and the disorganization of many American families today, many black families are finding it almost impossible to provide the kinds of supervision and guidance necessary to orient their children toward becoming adequate competitors for a better life in America. Only a casual observer of many black communities will note that too much valuable time of many black children is wasted in nonconstructive pursuits and unsupervised activities, if not neglected altogether.

Perhaps the one group in the population most keenly aware of this tragic phenomenon is our public schoolteachers. They almost never speak out publicly and seldom are they consulted for their views on the culturally deprived state of many black youths, or on the potential success or failure in life of their students. Yet, many of them can provide graphic details from their daily classroom experiences and contacts with parents that would produce a stunning and sobering education for many black children, their parents, and the community at large.

Most public school teachers can sometimes identify the potentially talented scholars and stars of tomorrow. More often, they can identify the early school dropouts, the prospective victims of early pregnancies, and very likely, the hardcore criminals of the very-near future. Quite often they can identify children who can be saved from a life of failure and despair with proper guidance and direction, if only they had an effective safety net to which they could refer them. To the extent that this is true, would it be naive and unrealistic for blacks to try to provide such a safety net—to supplement the efforts of many black families by establishing a nationally designed "Do You Want to Be Successful" program? Could not blacks urge their larger, stronger and most prestigious organizations to call upon the most able, resourceful, and diverse group of black and genuinely interested white and other Americans to attend a national conference? Could not such a conference plan and design a national organization and program for the personal development of many black, white, and other ethnic youths in the black community? Is it not plausible that such a program could be effectively coordinated through chartered local community-based organizations, providing an efficacious orientation to encourage, influence, and motivate many more youths in developing the following qualities?

1. A positive attitude towards learning and responding to proper adult leadership and supervision
2. A good set of practical, moral, and ethical values
3. Good manners and respect for themselves and others, particularly the elderly
4. Self-esteem
5. Reasonable articulation and writing of standard English

6. Responsible and dependable work habits—regular attendance and punctuality
7. Seriousness of purpose appropriate to the endeavor
8. Anti-drug-alcohol attitude with the willpower to abstain
9. Appealing, as opposed to offensive or negative personalities
10. Aspiration for positive goals

Do not all of these qualities more or less assure a competitive opportunity for a good education, good employment, self-sufficiency, and success in nearly any endeavor of life?

One might ask, but of what should such an orientation consist? Of course the answer to this question can be answered best by an aggregation of diverse experts and productive lay persons only after considerable discussion, consultation, deliberation, and planning by them. However, it would appear that a few of the many ideas and activities considered by them might include the feasibility of some of the following:

1. Chapter Meetings

   (a) Under knowledgeable supervision and direction, allow young chapter members to elect youth officers of the chapter and conduct their meetings in accordance with the *simple rules of parliamentary procedure.*
   (b) Teach them to respect one another in expressing their ideas, to respect the authority of the officers, and the officers to respect the membership.
   (c) Teach them the difference between subjects for committee work and subjects for plenary session discussions and reports.
   (d) Teach them the difference between *policy-making* and *executive functions* so that as adults more of them will know how to work more cooperatively and effectively in organizations, with a minimum amount of dissension and disorder.
   (e) Teach them to be sensitive about the use of incorrect English, and to be insensitive about being corrected.
   (f) Teach them to admire and respect achievement and positive qualities in adults and their peers, learn to

commend and praise one another when it is warranted, and to avoid becoming envious or jealous of such qualities in others. Correspondingly, teach them to be humble and avoid becoming conceited, big-headed, or braggadocious about accomplishments, personal attributes, praise, or popularity.

2. Black History

   (a) Commission history scholars to write a textbook of essentials of black history for junior and senior high school students.
   (b) Lobby state and local school boards and superintendents to select such textbooks and include them in the curriculum as a history course for credit. This should be easily accomplished in school districts with all black schools.
   (c) Plan for local chapters to have periodic lectures and discussions on black history so that more black youngsters will grow up knowledgeable and proud of their heritage, and not left confused and in search of an undefined identity.

3. Comparative Conduct Production

   (a) Using public school teachers as a main source, collect stories of their daily classroom experiences and contacts with parents, which demonstrate the *wrong* and *right* attitude of a child and/or its parents towards the teacher, education and classroom decorum.
   (b) Such collections could be submitted to volunteer playwrights to write into short stories and have junior or senior high school dramatic clubs constitute a cast for a stage production, a thirty or sixty-minute video or television production for viewing by pupils, parents, teachers, and the local community.
   (c) The specifics of such a production could present a comparative contrast of the rights and wrongs of table manners, how to dress for the occasion, how to behave

in public, and always, a comparative use of substandard and standard English.

4. Celebrity Recruitment

   (a) *Recruit* the voluntary presence and participation of celebrities of sports, theater, and the recording industry in all program activities as an incentive for attendance and full participation by the young people in program activities.

5. Travel

   (a) Group trips by automobile, bus, train, plane or boat to selected cities and geographic sites of great interest to broaden the experiences, intellectual curiosity, and aspirations of many children beyond their immediate and often very limited environment. Generally, the parents who often pay for expensive stereo equipment and designer clothes can pay the group fare for such trips. Otherwise, the community-based organizations can possibly engage in periodic fund-raising activities to help defray such expenses.

6. Selected Movie and Video Programs

   (a) Movie and video productions selected, recommended or furnished by the National Program Committee which all black youths should see which tend to inspire pride in their heritage and motivate them to aspire for positive goals with persistence in achieving them. Such productions are *Roots,* the three-part series of *The Different Drummer* (about blacks in the military), and *The Black Eagles* (the four-part video story of black pilots and airmen during World War II). Many of those military men and women are still alive and could be invited to the showing to further explain and answer questions about those interesting, encouraging, and courageous episodes of the black experience. Also, *Profiles in Courage* and many other productions addressing specific needs of the youth membership may be utilized.

7. Tutorial Programs

   (a) Tutorial programs particularly in English, mathematics, the sciences, microcomputer applications and technology, music (instrumental and voice), as well as the trade-crafts could be initiated. Local chapters may make an effort to work in a cooperative manner with the local school system in this regard.

8. Talent Bank and Counseling

   (a) Conduct talent searches and serve as a referral repository to which schoolteachers, church groups, and music teachers can refer gifted and promising youngsters with the potential to become scholars, or exceptional artists in the popular, classical, performing, and other fine arts— children who might not otherwise get the proper foundation for their development. The selected adult talent bank members may then utilize the full resources of the local and national organizations in directing such referred youths to the proper program or professionals for assistance (counseling, training, and financial help) for the development of their talent. Such referred youths may very well be the prospective and expanded replacements for the Percy Julians, Charles Drews, John Henry Johnsons, Count Basies, Duke Ellingtons, Stevie Wonders, Andre Wattses, Leontyne Prices, Grace Bumbrys, and Simon Esteses of tomorrow.
   (b) Establish national and local economic development committees to raise funds for the organization and to aid promising youths who lack financial means to further develop their talents. Such committees could also conduct lectures and discussion sessions on business, finance, and investments. They could introduce young people to our business world and explain how it works.

9. Wholesome Recreation

   (a) Chapter-sponsored disco dances under young adult supervision with the favorite popular music artists of youths.

10. Lectures

    (a) Recommended lectures on specific subjects by leading authorities recommended by the national and local adult program committee.

11. Modeling and Fashion Sessions

    (a) To be conducted by modeling and fashion instructors, emphasis should be on proper grooming and how to dress for the occasion, how to walk, sit, and how to always speak standard English.

12. Promote Study of Music

    (a) By providing musical instruments and establishing bands, orchestras, choruses and glee clubs; and by asking music instructors to initially contribute at least two or three hours a week instruction, and after a time, for a reasonable fee. When such participating youngsters learn what music they can make and what attention they receive, it is difficult to believe that many of them will not become proud enough to want to advance and become more; and that out of such community effort, the base would have been broadened to produce more talented personalities like Price, Basie and Whitney Houston.

13. Extensive Counseling Programs

    (a) Plan and present extensive programs, including films and lectures by physicians and other specialists on drug and alcohol abuse, AIDS, birth control, planned parenthood, and nutrition and proper diet to preserve health and control weight.

(b) Periodic sessions on parenting and private counseling for parents by highly qualified counselors. Example: Parents should be taught the adverse effects of youth overindulgence in television watching, and how to regulate and enforce the television viewing of their children.

14. Personal Development

(a) Having previously discussed the crucial state of personal development of black males, special attention should be given to the personal development of many of them. Drawing upon the expertise of such authorities as Robert Staples, Andrew Billingsley, Doris Wilkinson, Ronald Taylor, Alvin Poussaint, William Greer, Jewelle Taylor Gibbs, Price Cobb, and other professional and lay persons, a national program should be designed beginning at headstart age and continuing through high school to orient many more black males to goal-oriented, industrious, responsible, law abiding, and productive manhood. Such a program can and may be implemented concurrently with the total program for all youths, and may have as an adjunct, a Boy Scout troop established in each chapter or a combination of community chapters. Volunteer and recruited celebrity athletes and other trained black men and women who are willing to take the free adult scout training courses offered by the local Boy Scout headquarters would be prepared to serve as scout leaders. The principal objective of the Boy Scouts of America is to develop "character," "citizenship," and "leadership." This can be accomplished only with an adequate number of able and scout-trained adult leaders.

(b) Discuss the historical causes of conflict between the sexes and teach the girls and boys not to blame and antagonize each other over conditions which arose out of their unique history, but to work as partners and teammates to build good and stable relationships, including marriage.

174

15. Significance of the Black Church

   (a) Discuss the historical role of the black church in the life of the black struggle from slavery to the present. Explain how their strong ancestors and strong blacks today are so often able to endure, cope with, and overcome great economic and racial obstacles by the spiritual (religious) and fellowship nourishment they receive from church involvement; that the church has been the molding mentor of black group solidarity and collective strength throughout black history; that they should follow the teachings of God as Dr. King taught, to love all humankind in spite of their history, and to recognize an extended hand of many white people in friendship, love and cooperation; and that if they wish to be a part of their historical struggle and the ultimate successes; they should become a participating and supporting part of the church institution, and other organizations committed to democracy and equal opportunity. Church involvement is very often an important part of being happily successful.

16. Consumer Oriented Training and Other Services

   (a) Many young blacks are frequently the prey of fraudulent gimmickry or business trickery because of their lack of training and business experience, as well as for the want of some knowledgeable persons with whom they can consult. Thus, a committee of practicing lawyers, financial advisors, and sales persons may select and prepare an outline of consumer information covering business transactions and legal credit problems in which young blacks often become entangled at great losses and expense. Such problems and the effects of a debtor and sale of an automobile (new or used); also, landlord and tenant practices, signing negotiable papers, purchasing real estate, and understanding and avoiding deficiency debts and judgments.
   (b) Chapter sessions on consumer subjects may be conducted by sales persons, financial advisors and lawyers, to help

the young people avoid financial waste and setbacks.

(c) The Community or Regional Board of Governors can establish a cadre of volunteer and free consultative services with whom youths may *confidentially* consult, before making imprudent decisions and taking action upon them. Such services can include consumer advisors, psychologists, psychiatrists, gynecologists, urologists, the clergy, social workers and education counselors.

There are only several thousand other ideas out there waiting to be advanced in a national conference for the development of a program to be organizationally implemented.

Could not such an organization establish eligibility requirements for community or regional governing boards to oversee local community chapters to which an organization charter may be issued? Could not requirements for a charter include, among other things for approval, that a sponsoring organization:

1. Pledge to comply with the national constitution by-laws and regulations of the organization?
2. Provide the names and qualifications of the selected volunteer adult leadership committee of the sponsoring organization?
3. Provide evidence that the organization has a safe and adequate meeting facility (community hall, church hall, et cetera) to accommodate the recommended number of children and adult leaders?
4. Provide evidence that it has essential equipment to implement the program of the organization, such as wide-screen projection television, video cassette recorder, movie and slide projector and screen, an adequate public address system, and a computer to maintain records of youth membership, and to measure quality control of the program's effectiveness?
5. Provide evidence that it has adequate volunteer-trained security personnel to maintain order on the premises and to guard automobiles of participants while meetings and programs are in progress?
6. Provide a sufficient number of diverse and highly qualified adult volunteer leadership staffs and certify that the ratio of the adult leadership staff to youths complies with the ratio

recommended by the organization to assure effective control and administration of the program?

Volunteer Staff

Could not such a program be economically implemented through the selective use of able, dedicated, and responsible volunteers? Now more than ever before exists a large number of educated, trained, and comfortably situated retired blacks. Many of them are busy, and many are not for lack of something more challenging and meaningful to do. Many of them eagerly wish there was some way in which they could contribute their time, energy and resourcefulness to bring about a substantial improvement in the personal development of many young black girls and boys. Many blacks still in the work force wish there was some medium through which they could share their experiences and knowledge for the benefit of many black youths. Community-based chapters of such a national organization could very well constitute that medium or forum so badly needed and wanted by many concerned blacks.

Private Schools

The education of many American children today requires more than the standard educational structure provided by the average local public school system. Alternative educational structures, such as private boys, girls, and/or coeducational boarding schools and military academies may be the need of many children. Sometimes the needs of different siblings in the same family require different educational structures, and parents often have very few, or no alternatives to the standard local public school system.

Forty years ago, several such educational options were available to some black parents at a time when many of them could ill-afford to take advantage of them. Today many black parents with the financial resources in need of such private institutions find very limited or no appropriate options to serve the educational needs of their children. In fact, many white parents find themselves in the same situation.

Perhaps the national organization can consider the establishment of a few boarding schools and military academies made available to black and white students. Perhaps such institutions could be staffed by drawing heavily upon the high-quality experience of the young-retired schoolteachers (black and white) and the educational, technical, and administrative experiences of the young-retired men and women (black and white) of the military services. Many of these retirees would probably like to supplement their retirement benefits with a reasonable salary for work in a system where discipline is not a major problem and progress is a vivid reward. Many black parents today are willing and able to pay considerable tuition for an appropriately structured quality education so badly needed by the children of many of them.

One Way to Develop an Efficacy

Developing a comprehensive and effective efficacy would require the input and expertise of many professions and occupations including the recognized constructive experiences of many intelligent laypersons. Thus a well-planned and organized national conference could include the distinguished resourcefulness of the following:

1. Educators, school administrators and classroom teachers
2. Sociologists and social workers
3. Historians
4. Ministers of various denominations
5. Economists
6. Business educators, representatives and entrepreneurs
7. Cultural developers—musical, dance, and modeling directors
8. Scientists—biologists, physicists, chemists, and mathematicians
9. Engineers—mechanical, chemical, and electrical
10. Lawyers
11. Medical doctors
12. Military—retired generals, colonels, admirals, captains, and sergeants

13. Computer company representatives, programmers, and experts
14. Accountants (CPAs)
15. Secretaries
16. Recreation directors
17. Nutritionists
18. Athletic coaches
19. Many intelligent and constructive lay persons

The principal organizers and planners of such an organization could involve the most able and resourceful blacks of respected stature. Examples of a few such persons:

Lionel Newson, former president
Central State University

James Cheek, president
Howard University

Henry Ponder, president
Fisk University

Mary Hatwood Futrell,
President, N.E.A.

Marva Collins
Teacher, Chicago

Alphonso Pinckney, Robert Staples, Nathan Hare, Doris Wilkerson, Ronald Taylor, Jewelle Taylor Gibbs and William Julius Wilson
Sociologists

Alvin F. Poussaint
Psychiatrist

Kenneth Clark
Psychologist

John Hope Franklin
Historian

Jacqueline Fleming and Olive Taylor
Historians

Lerone Bennett, Jr.
Historian

Roger Wilkins
Professor of History

Eleanor Holmes Norton
Law professor

John Jacob, president,
National Urban League

Benjamin Hooks
Executive Director, NAACP

Edward Williams, Joint Center for Political Studies
Howard University

Marian Wright Edelman
Children's Legal Defense Fund

Faye Wattleton
Planned Parenthood

Rev. Leon H. Sullivan
O.I.C.

Dorothy Height
National Council of Negro Women

Rev. Arlene Churn
Rev. Samuel Proctor
Abyssinian Baptist Church

Rev. Vashti Murphy McKenzie
Baltimore, Maryland

Rev. Jesse Jackson
Coretta Scott King
Martin Luther King Center

Rev. Joseph Lowery
SCLC

Barbara Jordan
Former Congresswoman, Texas

Shirley Chisolm
Former congresswoman, New York

Andrew Brimmer
Economist

Joshua Smith
Entrepreneur

Susan Mayo
Doug Williams Foundation

James Weldon Norris, Director of Music
Howard University

D. Jack Moses, Former Director of Music
Cheyney, Pennsylvania

Simon Estes
Metropolitan Opera House

Arthur Mitchell
Harlem Dance Opera

Dorothy Maynor
Former concert soprano

Leontyne Price
Metropolitan Opera soprano

Billy Taylor
Orchestra leader and composer

Sarah Vaughn
Jazz singer

Stevie Wonder
Popular musician and composer

Arthur Walker, Jr.
Physicist

Col. Frederick Gregory
Astronaut

Coach Eddie Robinson (football)
Coach John Thompson (basketball)

The list of distinguished resource persons could also include the chief executive officer or representatives of black fraternities, sororities, and lodges, the National Council of Negro Women, the National Bar Association (an association of black lawyers), and National Medical Association (an association of black physicians), and members of the board of directors of several business corporations. The National Urban League and the NAACP could certainly be consulted on efforts to identify and locate numerous resource people (black and white), as well as in planning and organizing such an important national conference. Should such an undertaking ever occur, it should be very soon, before many of these distinguished people of stature pass from the active scenes of life.

After the receipt of reports of the various workshops conducted by the most able and resourceful leaders, a national executive board or committee could be selected to plan and develop, over a designated period of months, a comprehensive program to be implemented nationally and locally. Very able lawyers of the executive committee could draft the national constitution and by-laws, regulations, and requirements for community or regional governing boards, as well as guidelines for the local chartered chapters. They may also recommend the tax status of the organization and advise the board or committee on other relevant legal matters and procedures.

Participants in the initial national conference could be asked to return to a second conference scheduled several months later to ratify the constitution, by-laws, and the planned program. Possibly some black and other American corporations may volunteer to underwrite the sponsorship of such conferences. Otherwise, blacks may be willing to pay their individual share of the costs for such a conference. After the national organization and program are extensively promoted nationally, nearly every black church and community organization in the country would probably be begging for a local charter of such organization and its program.

Organization Staffing

Each community or regional governing board or committee could consist of the most able, personable, dedicated, and reliable persons in the community or region. Each member should have a genuine belief in the objectives and procedural operation of the program. The regional or community governing boards or committees could review the application and facilities, as well as meet and talk with a prospective volunteer staff of an applicant organization for sponsorship and recommend approval or disapproval of a charter to such organization. The regional or community governing board or committee could remain the overseer of the local chapters of the organization to assure that the program is being carried out in accordance with its objectives and procedures.

Local organizations seeking sponsorship of a chapter could select the most resourceful, respected, personable, and dependable citizens in the community who are genuinely interested in the program and are capable of working with adults and young people with a reasonable degree of harmony. They could solicit the continued support and participation of admired celebrities in the sports and entertainment world as helpers and provide incentives for young people to affiliate and fully participate in the scheduled program. Efforts could be made to have a helping job for every black who can make a constructive contribution to the successful execution of the program. Adult participation could be so abundant that the ratio between youth members and adult staff volunteers would remain small to permit a climate of affectionate intimacy and control.

Leadership Commitment

In selecting adult volunteers, each adult could be asked to file an application for participation, and if selected, sign a specially prepared agreement that he or she agrees with the program as designed and pledges to comply with its guidelines and to give the requested two or three hours a week of services for a period of three or five years; that he or she agrees to attend and participate in a special orientation on the objectives and rules and regulations of the program, and also to attend an initial and occasional joint orientation meeting of adult leaders, youth members, and their parents. All adult leaders could be urged to know each child by name and manifest a genuine and affectionate interest in all youth members.

Youth-Parent Commitment

Youths interested in the program may be asked to complete a specially prepared application for membership signed by them and their parents or acting guardians, pledging that both youth and parent or guardian agree to attend the initial youth-parent orientation meeting; and that if accepted for membership, the youth agrees to meet the regular time and attendance requirements of the chapter. On the same application, the parents or guardians can pledge to support the programs of the organization and cooperate with the child and adult leaders of the organization.

At the initial joint-orientation meeting, which would include adult leaders, youths, and their parents or guardians, organization leaders could explain the objectives of the organization and what is expected of each youth member and their parents. It could be made clear that participating adult leaders are volunteering their valuable time and resourcefulness because of their genuine interest in the personal development of each child; and that in order to remain in the program, each child must meet the regular attendance requirements, respect all adult leaders and their fellow youth members, and comply with the rules and regulations of the organization. Youth members who do not so comply should not be allowed to remain in the program.

In essence, each community chapter will have to try to be to youths of today the network that the YMCA, YWCA, boys clubs, church schools, and other groups were to earlier generations of young blacks. That is, a supplemental parent to some children, a reinforcing partner to the school system, and to children, a rendezvous for recognition and affection. Chapter staff members should constitute a set of worthy images for youths to emulate. It is conceivable that out of such a social climate, many young people will have met adults and peers who have made a permanent and positive influence on their attitude and aspirations for life.

Perhaps after middle-class blacks have been presented with such a challenge and summons for assistance, one might be able to credibly state whether or not they are sincerely interested and concerned with the welfare of less fortunate blacks. Until such time, it would appear that they are.

Prospective Results

If such a national efficacy is ever established and seriously implemented in one form or another, blacks and the nation will begin to recognize more young blacks manifesting an appreciation for themselves as proud Afro-Americans. More of them will be able to relate their historical past to the present. They will have developed a secure sense of self worth. Just as they understand and appreciate the words and tune of "America The Beautiful," they will know and appreciate the words, meaning, and music of the Negro National Hymn (Hymn of Dedication), which so aptly describes their ethnic history:

Lift Every Voice and Sing

Lift every voice and sing, till earth and heaven ring,
Ring with the harmonies of Liberty;
Let our rejoicing rise, high as the listening skies,
Let it resound, loud as the rolling sea.
Sing a song full of the faith that the dark past has taught us,
Sing a song full of the hope that the present has brought us,
Facing the rising sun of our new day begun,
Let us march on till victory is won.

Stony the road we trod, bitter the chastening rod,
Felt in the days when hope unborn has died;
Yet with the steady beat, have not our weary feet,

Come to the place for which our fathers sighed;
We have come over a way that with tears has been watered,
We have come treading our path thro' the blood of the slaughtered;
Out from the gloomy past, till now we stand at last,
Where the white gleam of our bright star is cast.

God of our weary years, God of our silent tears,
Thou who has brought us thus far on the way;
Thou who has by thy might, led us into the light,
Keep us forever in the path we pray.
Lest our feet stray from the places our God where we met thee,
Lest our hearts, drunk with the wine of the world, we forget thee;
Shadowed beneath thy hand may we forever stand,
True to our God, true to our Native Land.
   —James Weldon Johnson and J. Rosamond Johnson[*]

When Martin Luther King, Jr., spoke of "freedom," he envisioned neither panacea nor ultimate utopia. He appeared to have perceived "freedom" as an opportunity to develop one's potential to the maximum, along with the assumption of responsibilities which go with opportunities—a fair opportunity to compete for chosen endeavors, and an opportunity to eliminate injustices through democratic processes.

Once efficaciously oriented, many more young blacks will be motivated to pursue worthy goals and exploit opportunities for continued personal development, quality education, training, and gainful employment. A substantial majority of them will be able to cope with, overcome, or eliminate racial obstacles in their paths of progress. Most of them will not be influenced by anyone or by their circumstances to indulge in drugs or excessive use of alcohol. A significant number of them will be working as teammates and partners in black male-female relations and marriage. Many will be assuming active membership in, or support of, organizations with positive objectives for improving humankind. Virtually all of them will swell the ranks of law-abiding, industrious, self-sufficient and successful young Americans, while the numbers among the wayward, lawless, dependent, and destitute are noticeably reduced. Most of them will be invincible in pursuing their goals, and within a few years, the progress of blacks in general will be significantly accelerated amidst the ebb tide of racial repression. Essentially, all of such youths will fully understand and appreciate the meaning and the mission of the concluding words of Martin Luther King's famous "I Have A Dream" speech: *Free at last, free at last, thank God Almighty, free at last.*

Index

Black Muslims Sect, 139
Blacks, 37
Bloody Sunday, 139
B'Nai Brith, 133
Bohemians, 90, 95
Bolling *et al.* v. Sharpe *et al.*, 126
Bond, Julian, 133
Booker T. Washington High School, 61, 62
Boston, MA, 5, 140
Boy Scouts of America, 174
Boy Scout Troup, 174
Boyton v Virginia, 134
Briggs *et al.* v. Elliott *et al.*, 124, 125
Britain, 1
British, 48, 49
Bronx, NY, 97
Brooklyn College, 116
Brooke, Senator Edward, 61
Brown, 126, 127, 129
Brown, Chapel, 141
Brown, *et al.* v. Board of Education of Topeka, KS, 56, 59, 125
Brown, John, 32
Brown, Justice, 55
Brown, "Tony," 61
Bumbry, Grace, 172
Bureau of Census, 56
Bureau of Refugees, 42

C

Calhoun, A.W., 10
Calloway, Cab, 68
Camden, SC, 62
Camp Lejeune, NC, 71, 100
Canada, 31, 32
Caribbean, 1
Caribbean Island, 3
Carlton, Stephen, 7
Carnegie Corp, 77
Caroline County, VA, 142
Carter, Robert L., 120, 122
Cartwright, Samuel W., 29
Catastrophic social crisis, 149
Catholic, 132
Caucasian, 11, 35

Caucasoid, 11, 12
Central High School in Little Rock, AR, 130
Chance, William, 123
Chaney, James, 138
Charleston, SC, 32, 35, 37, 52, 62
Charleston, W. VA, 61
Chicago, IL, 113, 115, 116, 132
Chicago Tribune, 95
Chinese, 95
Christian, 6, 8, 9, 24
Civil Rights Act of 1865, 44
Civil Rights Act of 1875, 48
Civil Rights Act of 1964, 66, 138
Civil Rights Act of 1965, 142
Civil Rights Clause, 90
Civil Rights Coordinating Council of Federated Organizations, 137
Civil Rights Division, 142
Civil Rights Movement, 43
Civil War, 37, 41, 46, 52, 71
Claflin, 42
Clarendon County, SC, 124
Clark College in Atlanta, 42, 43
Cobb, Price, 174
Code of Ethics of the NAREB, 90
Coleman, William, 124
Colonists, 14
Colored, 64, 65
Colored Cumberland Presbyterian, 43
Colored Methodist Episcopal, 43
Colored Primitive Baptist, 43
Columbia law graduate, 116
Columbia, MO, 112
Columbia, SC, 97
Command assignment, 99
Commission on Civil Rights, 142
Committee on Govt. Contracts, 86
Community Chest, 88
Concerned Black Men, 163
Concord, NC, 62
Confederate, 37, 41, 48
Congress, 31, 34, 44, 45, 46, 47, 49, 50, 89, 136, 138, 140, 142, 143
Congress of Industrial Organization, 120

190

191

Irish, 95
Irving, Washington, 35
Italian, 56
Italians, 95
Ivy League, 60

J

Jackson, Jesse, 133
Jackson, Jimmy Lee, 139
Jackson, MI, 135
Jamestown, VA, 4, 6
Japanese, 95, 102
Japanese-American Citizens League, 120, 121
Jayhawkers, 46
Jefferson City, MO, 112
Jenkins, Howard, 110
Jewish Anti-Defamation League, 132
Jewish Harvard law scholar, 109
Jews, 91, 95
"Jim Crow," 48, 54, 129, 136, 139, 158
Johnson, Henry, 172
Johnson, James Weldon, 110
Johnson, Judge of AL, 140, 141
Johnson, Mordecai, 109
Johnson, Pres. Andrew, 43, 44
Johnson, Pres. Lyndon, 140, 141, 167
Justice Department, 142

K

Kansas, 36, 126
Kansas City, KS, 84
Katzenbach, Atty. Gen. Nicholas, 135
Kennedy, John F., 135, 136, 137, 167
Kennedy, Mrs., 137
Kentucky, 5, 20, 32, 37, 54
King, Coretta Scott, 133
King Cotton, 10
King, Dr. Martin Luther, Jr., 129, 130, 133, 135, 136, 139, 174
King of England, 1
Klansman, 141
Knights of White Camelia, 47
Knox, Frank, 100

Korea, 101, 102
Korean, 101
Ku Klux Klan, 46, 47, 48, 113, 135, 138, 139, 141

L

Latin America, 147
Latins, 91
Lawson, Belford V., 111, 122
Legal Defense Fund, 109
Lewis, John, 132
Liberia, Africa, 99
Lieutenant Gilbert, 101
Lincoln, Abraham, 37, 41, 43
Lincoln Memorial, 136
"Lintch's Law," 26
Lithuanians, 90
Liuzzo, Mrs. Viola Gregg, 141
Lord Dunmore, 48
Louisiana, 5, 15, 26, 29, 36, 37, 45, 51, 55
Lovings, 142
Loving v. Virginia, 142
Lowery, Joseph, 133
Lucy, Autherine, 130, 136

M

MacArthur, Gen. Douglas, 101, 102
MacArthur's Far East Command, 103
Macrostructural, 156
Malcolm X, 139
Margold, Nathan, 109, 110, 112
Marine Corps, 71, 99, 100
Marshall, Thurgood, 101, 102, 103, 109, 110, 111, 113, 115, 116, 117
Maryland, 5, 32, 37, 112, 113, 114
Maryland Law School, 111
Maryland Supreme Court, 111
Massachusetts, 4, 61
Master's, 26
Mather Academy, 62
McLauren, G.W., 120, 121
"Mecca," 138
Meharry Medical School, 59

197